CONTENTS

ACKNOWLEDGEMENTS

I wish to thank Ipswich Town Football Club for giving me the opportunity to work with all the young children and academy players at the club over the last 16 years. Without access to these players and the hands on experience working with them I would certainly not have been able to help write this book.

I would like to thank all the coaches I have worked with, especially George Burley, Tony Mowbury, Willie Donachie, Bryan Klug and Steve Foley, for making me a better conditioning coach. By talking about their experiences they have opened my mind up to the ways of soccer.

Simon Thadani

I would like to thank the many managers and coaches who I have worked with over the years (over twenty managers and thirty coaches). I have learnt many things in the game, good and bad, but my biggest lesson is that you find people and players' attitudes change through the good and bad days. It has taught me to persevere through the tough times, which made me a better person and coach. Tough times never last but tough people do!

Steve Foley

I'd like to thank Simon Thadani for the opportunity to be involved in this project. I'd like to acknowledge the continuing faith, support and encouragement that my husband and family give me in my work that makes this book possible.

Alison Byard

FOREWORD

If you read the papers and watch sports channels, you'll no doubt hear all sorts of debates these days about the influx of 'ready-made' players from abroad coming into the English game at the expense of 'homegrown' talent. The truth is that every league club has an academy largely made up of the best young British talent available, and in those clubs and academies are working some of the best coaches around, who develop the attitudes and skills these youngsters need to make it in the game.

I was lucky enough to work with such a coach – Steve Foley – when I was a young player at Norwich City in the 90s. The reason Steve's coaching works so well is because his approaches and drills, many of which are in this book, are tailor-made to kids at different ages and stages of development, and are the result of years of experience and 'trial and error'.

Of course, some of the trainees in academies are much younger these days than I was when I was at Norwich, and now Steve is applying his wisdom and coaching skills to kids of all ages down the road at Ipswich Town. He's lucky enough to work with conditioning coach Simon Thadani, part of the coaching team which helped with the development of players like Darren Bent and Kieron Dyer, who've gone on to Premier League and international success, and current young players like Danny Haynes and Owen Garvan. Ipswich's academy is still a fund of fine talent now being seen in the club's side, in no small part thanks to Simon and Steve's unique blend of coaching.

Kids' Football Fitness is all you need to make kids' football coaching and development fun, safe and productive, at whatever level of the game you are involved. Ali Byard's handy nutrition tips and advice complement the coaching and conditioning aspects perfectly to give you the tools to design your own complete programme for kids of all ages.

I have no hesitation in recommending this book, as much of the coaching advice and information here is what gave me the tools as a youth player to go on and make my name in the best league in the world and for my country.

Craig Bellamy, West Ham and Wales striker

INTRODUCTION

The aim of this book is to give you as the coach, teacher or enthusiastic helper a complete overview, under one cover, of what is required to teach football skills and techniques to young players, to introduce them to the physical demands of the game and to teach them the importance of nutrition. Although these are often viewed only as three separate components, they are very much interlinked. See the box below for a simple example of the knock-on effect when one component fails.

Before we detail what's in this book and how to use it, and look at the

CASE STUDY

We had two players at the academy, Player A and Player B. Both went through phases of poor concentration, listlessness and lack of energy. When we talked to them about their lifestyles, it turned out that they were both spending a lot of their free time in fast food restaurants and not eating regular meals. Player A was not drinking enough fluids, either before training or during sessions. Player A quickly remedied the situation by cutting out burgers and drinking noticeably more of the isotonic drinks we had on the training pitch. In no time he was more energetic, getting to the ball early, dribbling, making good passes and scoring goals. He was also a much happier member of the academy. Player B did not take the same advice on board and carried on with the burger regime, and we saw no improvement. Incidentally, the club released him soon afterwards.

enjoyment you should get from coaching and playing the game, we would like to discuss briefly the current social climate and how football, or any other sport, can reverse the worrying trends being seen more frequently in young people.

The subject of kids' health, fitness and body image has become an increasingly talked-about topic in recent years, and it seems there is some sort of new warning every week! Bad eating habits and sedentary lifestyles, aggravated by increased watching of television, computer games and the current social 'fear factor', have all combined to create serious and worrying concerns about the health of our children now. There is also a great deal of conflicting information for parents to digest. For example, the manufacturers of one of the world's bestselling computer consoles have suggested that using the console with certain games requires such physical activity with the controller that it reaps physical benefits to the user, whereas preliminary testing by scientists has suggested that such games offer little more calorie-burning or cardiovascular activity than other sedentary activities. So will people think that a console can replace the kind of benefits kids get from an afternoon of fresh air in the park?

We are not here to make judgements about anyone's lifestyle choices – but of concern to us is how all this will affect their health in the future and who will be setting the standards in future years! Though we are professionals, coaching and advising professional footballers on a daily basis, we are also involved on the ground with a lot of community projects that have allowed us witness with our own eyes the changing trends and rise of health problems in ordinary youngsters, far removed from the regimes now implemented in football club academies.

This is where football (or indeed any other sport) can be so important in helping reverse the trends. Well-organised, structured, safe football sessions that create an environment for learning, and an atmosphere of fun and enjoyment where the children have a chance to fall in love with playing the game, will guarantee they return for more and more. By simply doing this you will have a positive effect on their present and future lifestyle. *Get them active and the rest will take care of itself.*

Yes, football is about teaching the game, learning new skills, scoring goals, coaching basic conditioning methods and learning about nutrition, but the hidden benefits are sometimes forgotten too easily. We believe we have a bigger responsibility to use our knowledge and influence as coaches to achieve these benefits. What better side-effect of football could there be than healthy, happy kids?

The point we have already made – and will reiterate – is that football is fun, and the younger your players, the more fun it must be. For example, we suggest that the conditioning components you will find in Chapter 2 should not be introduced until kids are at least nine, and that fun warm-ups and basic drills, as found in Chapters 1 and 3, should be the key until young players have at least mastered the basics and are accustomed to football in general. This is for developmental reasons, both psychological and physical.

But what we do aim to show you in this book is that developing a structured programme including conditioning should not make it seem daunting, either to a coach or, worse, to the kids themselves. Football training is not a boot camp!

The theories and drills you will find in this book have been tried and tested at the highest level of professional football so that they can be used by everyone, from pro sessions at that level down to grassroots Saturday training at your local park. All you need is the ability to adapt as and when necessary, depending on whom you are coaching.

> You only get out what you put in, so if you want to improve, be patient. It takes time and effort, but always enjoy what you do.
> *Richard Naylor, 350 Premiership and Championship games, Ipswich Town*

Chapter 1 explains the importance of warm-ups before training and cool-downs for afterwards, with advice and golden rules for warming up with young players. Ten warm-ups follow, five without and five with a ball.

Chapter 2 introduces the four 'S's' – the crucial aspects of conditioning, namely Strength, Suppleness (Flexibility), Stamina and Speed. Ten drills accompany each component of conditioning that you can incorporate in your coaching programme. Each of these particular drills has a memorable drill name so the players can identify which one is which, and you can perhaps maintain more of a sense of fun when a ball is not involved.

In Chapter 3, we build on the basis of the conditioning components above with a selection of our best 'tried-and-tested' coaching drills. We know from personal experience that the variety in these drills will keep your young players interested and will increase their skill as footballers while they're having fun. Each drill has a suggested age range for which it is suitable, based on children's development, which will allow you to mix and match with your programme.

Chapter 4 explains the basic forms of energy in foods and their role within the body and for sport, then explains how different foods are classified and what they contain that is beneficial and potentially harmful. Later in the chapter, there is plenty of advice on what young players should be eating, and when, and tips on hydration, packed lunches for awaydays, when to allow takeaways and much more.

In Chapter 5, we show you how to combine everything in Chapters 2–3 to create your own special programme suited to the young players you coach, and there are some more pointers and advice about what to consider when you are building your programme.

Appendix 1 details sample session plans and programmes based on the information in Chapters 2–3. Appendix 2 contains sample menus for rest days, matchdays and training days based on advice in Chapter 4. Appendix 3 contains two case studies of change to nutritional and dietary habits, and finally Appendix 4 has guidance on injury treatment, both immediate treatment and for long-term rehabilitation.

Occasionally when describing a player, we will refer to that player in general terms as 'he'. This should be taken to mean 'he' or 'she' as appropriate.

1 THE WARM-UP AND THE COOL-DOWN

Why warm up?

We warm up to prevent injury and prepare the body for exercise, so warm-ups are an integral part of any session and must not be done on an ad hoc basis. Some of these are also appropriate as cool-downs (also known sometimes as warm-downs). See more about cool-downs on page 4.

Is warming up with kids different?

The need to warm up for young players is just as important as warming up for adults, and by starting each of your coaching sessions with a warm-up you will lay solid foundations for the future, making it part of the education of players for their adult years. However, you need to take the following factors into consideration when you are conducting a warm-up session with young players:

Concentration span
It is a psychological fact that the younger the child, the shorter their attention span. So, keep the drills short with natural breaks, and try to make sure that they are varied and as fun as possible. To do this without a ball is not easy at times, so arranging groups and layouts in patterns (circles, squares, triangles etc.) and using equipment can be very useful (see drills themselves for what we mean). This stops kids getting bored and keeps their interest, particularly if you do the drills in a different order or a different way each time you have a session.

How long?
Your warm-up will typically last eight to 10 minutes (depending on the weather – see Golden Rules on page 3), allowing you to fulfil all its requirements (see box)

Charlton's Donnique Sinclair-Chambers stretches before a game

before the main session begins. Younger groups should have longer breaks between activities during this introductory period so you don't overwork them before the rest of the session. Taking a little longer to explain things to younger age groups will help you achieve this.

WHAT WILL YOUR WARM-UP ACHIEVE?

- Raises players' heart rates in a controlled fashion over a couple of minutes so that more oxygen reaches muscles and increased bloodflow warms tissues
- Improves mobility with multi-directional work
- Increases flexibility through stretches, ideally dynamic work (depending on age group)
- Gets players in the right frame of mind for the main exercise session by raising tempo with fun games, with or without a ball.

How to structure the warm-up

Like many things in football, how you do a warm-up has been debated for many years. In our opinion, for kids it has to be a mixture of activities with and without a ball.

Doing drills without a ball varies the warm-ups, and including aspects of conditioning (quick feet, agility or reaction work) brings different types of fun into the session. In our experience, children enjoy the variety – if they know what is coming, and it is something they don't enjoy, they sometimes become bored. As we said earlier, using your imagination is key.

If your time with the players is limited, using a ball gives them a chance to get used to having it at their feet and they become comfortable with it before the main session begins. Warming up with a ball, like jogging and running, will increase heart rates, but ensure you stick to the basic skills for this. Always start slowly with a ball and don't make the work too intensive.

A top coach we worked with once commented to us that a warm-up can be the most important part of the session for a coach, as it gives you a feel for what

TEN GOLDEN RULES FOR WARM-UPS

1. The purpose of a warm-up is to prevent injury and prepare the body for the main session
2. Before you start the warm-up, check that nobody is carrying any injuries or illness
3. The younger the players are, the more fun it should be
4. With younger players, the warm-up should have a combination of walking and jogging so as not to over-exert them
5. Remember that younger players are less able to concentrate, so do drills in short bursts
6. The younger the players are, the more supple and flexible they should be, which should be reflected in the drills you choose
7. The older the players are, the more educating about good habits there should be
8. The warmer the weather is, the shorter the warm-up can be. The colder it is, the longer it should be
9. Make sure players have had a drink and are kept hydrated, especially in warm weather
10. Always finish a warm-up with a fun game or relay.

the players are going to be like for the rest of the session and that the warm-up sets the standard. With young players, if the warm-up is well planned and structured, and you are motivated as a coach, it tends to rub off. Kids are not stupid – they pick up on things very quickly!

Suggested combinations of the warm-up drills that follow in this chapter on pages 6–19 can be found in the sample sessions in Appendix 1 on pages 184–6.

Cool-downs

Cool-downs (often referred to as warm-downs) are the phase of training during which the body adapts and recovers from training or a match. There are important physiological benefits to be gained by cooling down after a very hard training session or match (see below box on benefits).

Cool-downs should be an integral part of any training session, although they are often forgotten due to time restrictions and other considerations. Over the last 10 years working with professional players, we have noticed the different attitude to cool-downs that players from abroad seem to have compared to British players. Most overseas players seem to understand the importance of a good cool-down compared to the majority of their British counterparts, who can't wait to finish a cool-down and go off and do some shooting! The reason for this is the education of players at a very young age in schools and clubs abroad, which we have also been careful to instil into our players at the youngest age we can. We therefore hope you can see the importance of trying to educate the players at this young age to take it on board as much as they do the need to warm up.

WHAT ARE THE BENEFITS OF A COOL-DOWN?
Cool-downs allow the body systems to return to normal, so that:

- heart rate returns to normal gradually, in a controlled fashion
- gradual reduction of activity avoids blood pooling in active muscles and allows removal of waste products such as lactic acid
- bloodflow normalising and not pooling will avoid dizziness and fainting due to lack of blood to the brain
- active muscle cooling will prevent or reduce stiffness.

A cool-down with everyone gathered around in a calm atmosphere also gives the coach an opportunity to say well done to the players for the effort they put in during the session.

What should a cool-down comprise?

There are three basic stages to a cool-down:
· Lowering the heart rate in a controlled fashion. This can be done by slow jogging or a moderate walk for several minutes.
· Developmental stretching, mainly static stretching on the floor.
· Re-mobilisation – getting the players on their feet, walking around and shaking their legs and arms gently.

These stages will help achieve the aims detailed in the above box. As with warm-ups, see tips for programme design on the best way to choose stretches and structure your cool-downs.

The warm-up drills

Below are five drills for use without a ball and five for use with a ball. For more warm-up drills with a ball, refer to our tips for programme design (see Appendix 1) where we've included sample warm-ups using basic drills from Chapter 3 (see pages 106–15).

The drills in this section can be used with children of all ages, but please bear in mind that you do not want to overwork younger children, so it might be worth beginning drills with a walk, not a jog, and for activities to be done for less time until children are used to the drill.

You will only get out what you put in – like school classes, you will not learn or improve unless you are enthusiastic about what you are doing.
David Wright, former England U21 International with over 350 games in the Premiership and Championship

1.

Warm-up Drill
Magic Roundabout

Age group: All age groups
Purpose: Warm up without a ball, using a circle
Equipment: A dozen cones (if no centre circle)
Duration: 8–10 mins
Space: Centre circle of a pitch or a circle marked out with cones
Number of
participants: Minimum of 8

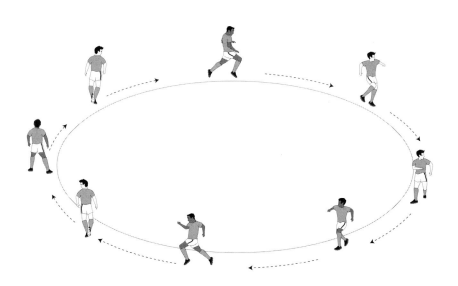

Easy jog around the circle, 1 min.

Introduce the following every 20 secs:
- Sidestepping
- Skipping
- Running backwards
- Zigzag running – 2 steps right, 2 left, 2 right, etc.
- Redo the above four actions in reverse order

Several dynamic stretches (see pages 49–58).

Jogging around circle in opposite direction, 1-2 mins:
- Changing pace
- Practising headers (jump in the air and do heading action)
- Zigzag running
- Stopping and starting

Stretch again.

FUN GAME

On coach's command (in any order), running:
- same direction forwards
- same direction backwards
- opposite direction forwards
- opposite direction backwards
- sidestepping inwards
- sidestepping outwards.

The players must react quickly to the coach's instructions, with the last player to react receiving a forfeit. Make this something fun, not 100 press-ups! See Appendix 5 on page 211 for some ideas.

2.

Warm-up Drill
Infernal Triangles

Age group: All age groups
Purpose: Warm up without a ball, using a square
Equipment: Five cones
Duration: 8–10 mins
Space: A square marked out 25 x 25 m
Number of
participants: Minimum of 8

Divide the players equally at points 1 and 2 (see diagram). Players starting at 1 jog to 3 and then 4, and then back to 1. Simultaneously, players starting at 2 jog to 4 and then 3, and then back to 2 and rejoin queue.

The aim is to be alert and aware of others in the square so as not to bump into anybody in the middle. Explain to players that their timing must be precise.

Once the players are jogging, introduce the following every 20 secs:
* Sidestepping
* Skipping
* Running backwards
* 2 steps right, 2 left, 2 right etc (zigzag)
* As above but backwards

Follow with several dynamic stretches (see pages 49–58).

Then continue with:
* Changing pace
* Practising headers
* Zigzag running
* Stopping and starting
Stretch again.

FUN GAME

Get players in the same starting positions and begin the jogging. When the first players of each group reach the middle of the square at point 5, they jump and give each other a 'high five'. The players then bounce off each other, so the player who started at 1 gives a high five, then jogs to 4, and then jogs back to 1. Player at 2 gives a high five, goes to 3 and then back to 2. When first players return to their groups, the next of each group goes.

Other commands you can give in the middle of the square are:
* 'low five'
* jump and touch each other's shoulders
* jump and touch each other's chest
* anything else you can think of – just use your imagination!

3.

Warm-up Drill
Harem Squarem

Age group:	All age groups
Purpose:	Warm up without a ball
Equipment:	Cones
Duration:	8–10 mins
Space:	A square marked out approx. 30 x 30 m
Number of participants:	Minimum of 8

Players jog gently around inside the square, avoiding bumping into each other, for 1 min. Then introduce the following every 20 secs:

- Sidestepping
- Skipping
- Running backwards
- 2 steps right, 2 left, 2 right etc. (zigzag)
- As above, but backwards

Follow with several dynamic stretches (see pages 49–58).

Then continue with:
- changing pace
- practising headers
- changing directions
- stopping and starting

Stretch again.

FUN GAME

While the players are jogging around the square in different directions shout a number, say three. The players then huddle up in groups of three. Any players without a group of three or the last group of three to react have to do a forfeit. Play this game several times.

4.

Warm-up Drill
Matching Pairs 1

Age group: All age groups
Purpose: Warm up without a ball
Equipment: None
Duration: 8–10 mins
Space: n/a
Number of
participants: Minimum of 8

Players are in two columns and in pairs as shown in the diagram. Take them around the pitch or training area, always keeping the formation. Introduce the following every 20 secs:
- Sidestepping
- Skipping
- Running backwards
- Zigzag running – 2 steps right, 2 left, 2 right etc.
- As above, but in reverse order.

Several dynamic stretches (see pages 49–58).

Then continue with:
- changing pace
- practising headers
- zigzag running (quicken tempo)
- stopping and starting.

Stretch again.

FUN GAME

As they are jogging or walking, give the players the following instructions. All the players have to do is the opposite of the instructions given!

COMMAND	ACTION
Jump up	Touch the floor
Swap positions	Stay the same
Right hand touch the floor	Left hand touch the floor
Change direction	Keep going in same direction

Each pair that gets it wrong receives a forfeit. You can also call out the actions in the right-hand column, with the respective action then in the left-hand column.

5.

Warm-up Drill
Matching Pairs 2

Age group:	All age groups
Purpose:	To develop quick feet
Equipment:	2 ladders, 8 small hurdles, 10 cones
Duration:	8–10 mins
Space:	Square laid out approx. 30 x 10 m
Number of participants:	Minimum of 8

Players are in two columns and in pairs. Working between the equipment, but not using it, players jog up and down for 1 min. Then introduce the following every 20 secs:

- Sidestepping
- Skipping
- Running backwards
- Zigzag running – 2 steps right, 2 left, 2 right etc.
- As above, but in reverse order.

Dynamic stretches.

Then, using the equipment, players:

- go through just the ladders 4 times
- in and out of the cones 4 times
- run with one foot between each hurdle 4 times.

Stretch again – use 3 or 4 different stretches.

FUN GAME

The fun game for this drill is a relay race. The first person from each group does quick feet through the ladders, runs in and out of the cones, does one foot between each hurdle action, then sprints back and touches the next team-mate in line, who then goes. Whichever group finishes last does a forfeit.

6. Warm-up Drill In and Out

Age group:	All age groups
Purpose:	Warm-up with ball
Equipment:	Balls, discs
Duration:	5–10 mins
Space:	30 x 30 m
Number of participants:	Various (2 or more)

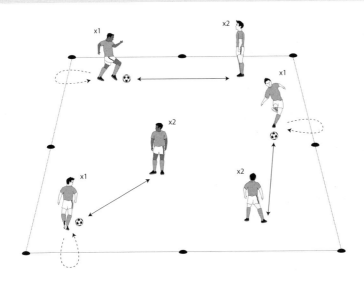

Players in pairs pass to each other. Once they have passed to their partner, they run outside the area and then back into the area again.

PROGRESSION
Get the players to jump in the air or bend down to touch the floor after passing the ball.

Start all drills slowly, and stop every 2–3 minutes to stretch. In the final minutes of the warm-up the drill can be at a higher tempo.

7.

Warm-up Drill
Lay it Back

Age group:	All age groups
Purpose:	Warm-up with ball
Equipment:	Balls, cones/discs/poles
Duration:	5–10 mins
Space:	10 m diameter circle
Number of participants:	5 or more

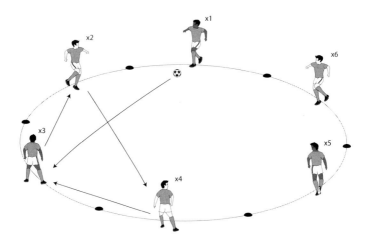

X1 passes to X3, who lays the ball to X2, who passes to X4, who lays the ball back to X3 and so on.

PROGRESSION
Add more balls.

Start all drills slowly, and stop every 2–3 minutes to stretch. In the final minutes of the warm-up the drill can be at a higher tempo.

8.

Warm-up Drill
Sides to Middle

Age group: All age groups
Purpose: Warm-up with ball
Equipment: Balls, cones/discs/poles
Duration: 5–10 mins
Space: 20 x 20 m square
Number of
participants: 6 or more

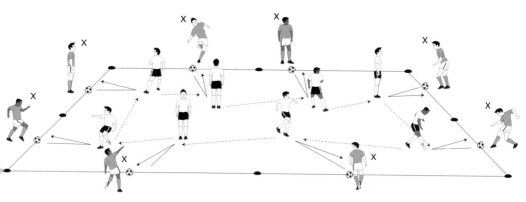

Each player (X) on the perimeter of the square has a ball. Players inside the area receive the ball and pass it back (one–two). They then run across to receive the ball from another player to continue the drill. After a certain time, e.g. one minute, swap the players over.

PROGRESSION
- Headers
- Volleys
- Chest, etc.

Start all drills slowly, and stop every 2–3 minutes to stretch. In the final minutes of the warm-up the drill can be at a higher tempo.

9.

Warm-up Drill
Three's a Crowd

Age group:	All age groups
Purpose:	Warm-up with ball
Equipment:	Balls, poles/cones/discs
Duration:	5–10 mins
Space:	20 x 20 m square
Number of participants:	6 or more

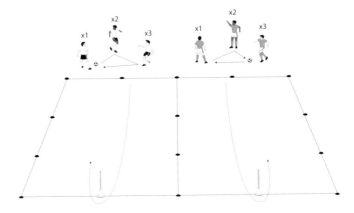

Players in groups of three give themselves numbers 1, 2, 3 and pass the ball to each other, keeping moving around in a circle.

On the coach's call, e.g. '2', all the 2s sprint round the far pole/disc/cone and back to pass and move again.

PROGRESSION

When going to the far disc do various exercises, e.g.

- full circle round the disc
- sideways run
- backwards run.

Start all drills slowly, and stop every 2–3 minutes to stretch. In the final minutes of the warm-up the drill can be at a higher tempo.

10.

Warm-up Drill
Pass and Run

Age group:	All age groups
Purpose:	Warm-up with ball
Equipment:	Balls, cones/discs/poles
Duration:	5–10 mins
Space:	20 x 20 m square
Number of participants:	2/4 or more

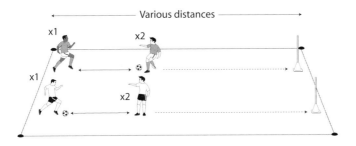

X1 passes back and forth with X2. After 10 passes X2 turns and runs to the far side of the area. X1 runs with the ball and meets up with X2 to continue the exercise for another 10 passes, then turns and runs to the far side of the area.

PROGRESSION

Passing with various parts of the feet, e.g. inside, outside.

Start all drills slowly, and stop every 2–3 minutes to stretch. In the final minutes of the warm-up the drill can be at a higher tempo.

2 INTRODUCING CONDITIONING TO YOUNG PLAYERS

At what age should children begin conditioning work?

Before we go on to talk about conditioning components, we would like to reiterate a point you have already read and that we will continue to repeat throughout this book: the younger the kids are, the more it should be about enjoying playing football for its own sake, having fun and falling in love with the game.

Once you have achieved this, from the ages of about seven years to nine years it should then be about teaching basic skills, techniques and good habits, and playing the game.

As the kids get older – we suggest from nine years old – start to introduce very basic conditioning components, educate them about fitness and nutrition, and get them doing basic drills appropriate to age, as shown in Chapter 3. We hope that even if you are coaching children as young as seven you will read this chapter on conditioning for interest, but we would advise you to think carefully about when you introduce these components, even if you have a skilful and enthusiastic bunch of players with obvious potential in your group.

In very simple terms, many of the basic conditioning benefits can be achieved by just training and playing football. Time is often limited, so ball work has to be the priority. As we mentioned in the introduction to this book, there is often a lack of access to kids as coaches, or a lack of time to play and train, say at school in PE lessons.

However, as your players get a little older, the basic four conditioning blocks – what we call the four 'S's' (Strength, Suppleness, Stamina, Speed) become

Republic of Ireland U21 defender Joe O'Cearuill uses his strength, suppleness and stamina to keep up with pacy England U21 forward Theo Walcott

more important and relevant, and time should be found to work on these, even if it's only for a few minutes each session.

Finally, as the children get beyond growth spurt (more about this on pages 27 and 28), do not underestimate the benefits of some hard physical work. By then, they will know that doing conditioning work will make you quicker and stronger, help your endurance (i.e. you'll last longer in a game) and make you more agile, but just as important, when players reach a certain age, are the mental benefits of working hard at the right time and place. This in turn will make the player mentally stronger. In our experience this creates a good work ethic, as they get to experience what hard work feels like in an environment that they enjoy – it gets them out of the comfort zone and they will soon understand why it is important to work hard occasionally in training. See box for examples you can give to a player who moans to you that there is no point in doing a particular drill. (Like we have already said, keep your sessions interesting – but be prepared for the inevitable voice of dissent even when everyone else is enjoying themselves.)

WHAT'S IN IT FOR ME?

'You're a striker. The game's nearly over and you're 2-0 up, so the team you're up against are playing a high line to try to keep the ball at your end and score to get back in the match. You and your marker (the last defender) are watching from the halfway line when the opposition's attack breaks down and your defence clears. As your midfield brings the ball forwards, your marker tracks you back, but as one of your team-mates delivers a diagonal ball forwards, you lose the defender with an instant burst of pace. Despite the defender accidentally clipping your heels as you disappear, you stay upright, continuing your run right up the pitch and picking up the ball in your stride, before deftly rounding the onrushing 'keeper to score in an empty net.'

Ask the player how he managed to do this. Can he tell you? If not, explain that because he had stamina, even in the latter stages of the game, he could still summon the speed he needed to outrun the defender, he had the suppleness in his muscles to instantly access his pace, and he had the strength to stay on his feet when he was clipped. He used his stamina to continue the run, and agility he learned through speed and stamina work to use his quick feet to beat the goalkeeper.

'You're a defender. It's 2-2 in a game against your closest league rivals. You could do with the three points but can't afford to lose. The manager has told everyone to push upfield to try for a winner, but you're the last man, marking their lone striker on the halfway line. Suddenly your attack breaks down and their defence clears. As their midfield brings the ball forwards, you track your man back. As one of his team-mates delivers a diagonal ball forwards, he sets off to run on to the pass. You keep pace with him, get in front of him and slide across to intercept the ball cleanly before he gets it, and you clear it for a throw-in, which your midfield deal with. The game ends.'

If your player needs telling how he achieved this, explain that because he had stamina, even in the latter stages of the game, he could still summon the speed he needed to keep up with the attacker, he had the suppleness and stamina in his muscles from multi-directional work to outrun and change direction to meet the ball, and he had the strength and suppleness to reach the ball on the ground without injuring himself or the other player, and the agility from the conditioning components to deliver the ball to safety without committing a foul which might have seen him red-carded.

With both scenarios, it is worth mentioning that aspects of conditioning encourage the kind of guile and quick thinking that both of these situations required, as well as the physical response, in order to succeed.

Conditioning for children and young adults

It is important that, as a coach, you have a basic knowledge of physiology, so that your awareness of the stages of children's development will make you a better coach in turn.

There have been huge developments in sports science in the past 10 years, and nowadays it is obvious from research and development that there are very significant physiological differences between fully-grown adults, young children and developing young adults. While it is true that coaches have probably always made allowances for younger players' lesser capability to complete drills, we now also have to consider the impact of each and every conditioning drill on the physical development of that young player. Coaches almost certainly didn't consider this in past years. Some senior drills will not help a young player develop, but, more importantly, they could actually have a negative impact on their development.

Another key issue that we have to bear in mind is that children develop at different ages, physically. Chronological age is not a perfect marker of physical maturity. We have seen many early developers have an advantage in football for that age group because of their size and strength. But often, they then stop growing and other players catch up, and therefore they lose one of their advantages when trying to be noticed.

This has to be taken into account when planning conditioning for young players – not only will you have to differentiate according to what position your player takes on the field, or the stage of the season, but also for a player's physical development. Whoever said coaching young players was the easy option was quite wrong.

The youth of today

Not every child will become an elite player, but if we help them to enjoy sport, we have no doubt that we can halt the disturbing trend towards obesity and the resulting poor health that we see in our children today. Let's look at some of the factors that affect fitness.

Factors that affect physical fitness with children

There is a degree of 'nature/nurture' with young people's physical fitness and abilities:

• **Genetics** – probably one of the biggest factors. How a number of children respond to training will be pre-derived and hereditary (see *body type*, below)

FIGURE 2.1 | **BODY TYPES**

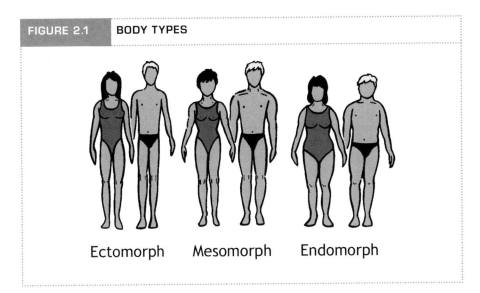

Ectomorph   Mesomorph   Endomorph

- **Lifestyle** – another big factor, but this one is influenced by what they do day to day, from walking to school or taking the dog for a walk to playing active sport at school several times a week. If they do little or no meaningful exercise, their initial response will be poorer
- **Age** – Capabilities change with age. Growth spurts may change body weight, co-ordination, and motor skills
- **Gender** – Obviously, development differs greatly between male and female
- **Body type** – Hereditary factors may influence physical capabilities and body shapes. For example, ectomorphs (taller people of lean build) cope better with activity requiring endurances. Endomorphs (shorter people of broader build) tend to develop earlier. Mesomorphs tend to be more athletic. See Figure 2.1 for illustrations of body type
- **Diet** – Healthy eating patterns provide sufficient energy for physical activity, in the right way at the right time for exercise. Also, we should not forget nutrients and vitamins to supplement these patterns. For much more on all of this, see Chapter 4
- **Current status** – Acquired conditions, from a cold to a calf strain, may affect a player's performance for that day
- **Attitude** – We have learned over the years that, even at a young age, attitude, desire, perseverance and motivation play a massive part in the enjoyment and fun children have, and this has a positive impact on their sporting development.

Defining age groups for conditioning

When developing conditioning programmes for young players, we typically use three groups, detailed in the below box. Remember the point made earlier in this chapter – children develop at different ages. See pages 28–31 and below for more on the physiological changes young players will be going through. It is not enough to say that all boys will have finished their main growth spurt by the age of 14. Nor can you say that boys and girls will develop at the same age – they do not. These groups are intended to aid your planning; but they are not a shortcut to avoid the hard work of developing programmes for individuals – you must read the below sections on the factors of development and differences between children and adults to plan safely and effectively. As we have already said, you need to make honest and careful judgements about the group you coach and their known or presumed abilities.

TABLE 2.1	KEY AGE GROUPS
Young children	7–9 years old
Pre-growth spurt (boys)	9–13/14 years old
Pre-growth spurt (girls)	10–12/13 years old
Post-growth spurt (boys)	13/14–16 years old
Post-growth spurt (girls)	12/13–16 years old

Young children

The only work we would advise with this age group is basic speed, agility and quickness work (see Speed drill 12, page 94) and the relay races (see speed drill 14, page 96), because these are fun activities without any issues about the players being too young. An idea of what to include is in the programme samples in Appendix 1.

Pre-growth spurt

At this age, the emphasis should be still on fun – let the children just get on with the game. All the aerobic and anaerobic work that they need to develop will be gained by playing football. Conditioning training will also be limited by time, as young children shouldn't exercise for prolonged periods. As this is the case, ball work still takes precedence.

However, adapted light strength exercises – with technique and posture high on the list of priorities – should be encouraged (see page 40). Proprioception work (see box below) and core stability work are important for balance, although children may find the science difficult to understand, let alone what benefits they will gain. It is very much about education at this early age – setting in place good habits that the young players will take with them for the rest of their lives. Some conditioning exercises, as we have discussed, can be detrimental to younger individuals going through changes as they develop. Even those exercises that don't harm a child's development and well-being may nevertheless still not be of any great help to them now, but to an extent they condition the player's mind to do them as a matter of routine later on when they will help their conditioning, so it's worth touching on them.

WHAT IS PROPRIOCEPTION?

Proprioceptors are sensory receptors in muscles, tendons, joints and the inner ear. The body uses proprioceptors to establish its position and relay messages to the central nervous system and help the body remain balanced. Our ability to do so is called *proprioception*. If we had no proprioceptors, we would be unable to walk or move in a co-ordinated way. An example of developed proprioception in action is the involuntary movement of the upper body that you make to try to stop yourself falling if you step on a patch of ice or slip in the shower.

Here are examples of the type of exercises that pre-growth spurt children should be doing with carefully judged frequency (see pages 36–46 for details of these exercises):
- box/knee press-ups
- adapted star jumps
- simple burpees
- dorsi raisers
- adapted sit-ups.

Some sprint drills are also good at this age, as long as the sessions are short and the emphasis is on technique, with plenty of rest between efforts. Dynamic stretching routines can also be adopted during these sessions. See Appendix 1 on pages 184–6 for advice on what to put in your conditioning programmes and for specific details and suggested drills.

Post-growth spurt

Again, the education element is important with this age group. If you have coached them from a younger age, players should by now have developed sound training habits, so you can move on to laying down foundations for the principles of conditioning. This is the age to introduce conditioning and techniques as components in their own right.

WHAT IS A 'BLEEP TEST'?

A bleep test requires a player to run between 2 lines while a machine bleeps at ever more frequent intervals. The object is to last as long as you can. As a season progresses, a player's fitness should improve and if they were not beating their previous 'bleep' score they soon will!

Bleep tests can be purchased from any main sports supply company.

Players can also continue to work on adapted first-team conditioning drills such as speed relay races and 'bleep tests'. Not only does this help motivate the players but it also prepares those who will go on to train at senior level.

The factors of children's development and physiology on planning conditioning

We have now suggested to you the suitable levels of conditioning and physical work for certain broad age ranges, but it is worth discussing development and different physiology between adults and children in some more detail.

There are many books and resources dedicated to physiology and the effects of training on a child's physical development. This is obviously a specialist subject and so we cannot cover everything in this chapter. Rather, the following is intended to give you an overview of the key points that you should bear in mind so that your programme will not cause the children in your care any developmental problems.

Anatomy

- **Ossification** (hardening of bones through deposit of calcium salts) is typically not completed until 18–20 years old, and in some adults as late as 25.
- **Bone growth** is dramatically affected by the growth spurt (generally this occurs in girls at 10–12 and boys 12–14). This may cause decrease in co-ordination, susceptiblity to injury, and consequently a lack of enthusiasm and loss of form.
- **Basic body types** – Endomorphs and mesomorphs typically develop earlier and therefore stop growing earlier, meaning that the remaining ectomorphs, who develop later, catch up. See more on body types on page 25.

Preventative measures to avoid 'growth-related injuries'

- Avoid excessive training loads (especially during the growth spurt).
- Remember that there can be up to a four-year development difference within the same age group.
- Encourage children to stretch at an early age (see more on stretching on pages 48–58).
- Avoid too much high-impact work such as plyometrics or heavy 'bounding' sessions.

Skills development and learning styles

- Children's neuro-muscular systems are not fully developed, so coordination. can be difficult. To stimulate development introduce SAQ and similar drills, such as Speed drill 12 on page 94
- Their reaction time is slower.
- Memory and concentration skills are not fully developed, so they lose concentration and can become bored quickly.
- Simple games such as the one on page 81 will help develop coordination and balance, which can make a good player a great one.

Physiological differences between adults and children

- Children have smaller hearts and lungs in proportion to body size.
- The surface area of the lungs is less, so the rate of diffusion of gases is lower.
- Children have a lower stroke volume (amount of blood pumped per beat).
- Children have a higher heart rate at rest and during exercise.
- Children breathe faster than adults.

As with other signs of development, such as growth spurt, there can be huge differences in body size, muscle mass and heart volume between children of the same age.

Children's anaerobic system

This does not develop until after puberty, as until this stage children have not fully developed the necessary forms of energy storage and use (see box for details).

Before puberty, children who can run easily are simply 'good runners' who are able to use aerobic energy (energy derived from oxygen in the bloodstream via the lungs) effectively, but with no real preference for types of running, whether sprinting or endurance.

ENERGY FORMS AND BY-PRODUCTS

- **Creatine** – Creatine is perhaps best known as a powdered supplement used by athletes for rapid muscle gain to improve performance, but it occurs naturally in foods such as beef, tuna and salmon, though in relatively small quantities. Creatine phosphate (or phosphocreatine) is stored in the musculoskeletal system to provide an instant burst of energy to the muscles. Children's capacity to store creatine is very limited, so it is of little practical use until muscle development increases at puberty. You must not give children creatine supplements, as it will be of no help and may cause damage. Such supplements are only for use by adult athletes with fully-developed musculoskeltal systems.
- **Glycogen** – The form in which carbohydrates from food are stored as energy in the muscles and liver until needed.
- **ATP (adenosine triphosphate)** – ATP is the energy found in muscle cells, drawn from stored energy sources such as phosphocreatine and glycogen, that keeps them functioning so that muscles contract.
- **Lactic acid** – The by-product of the process in which glycogen is converted into energy by muscle cells. Too much lactic acid causes muscle fatigue, but this diminshes when oxygen reaches the muscles and the majority of it returns to the muscle tissue as useable glycogen.

After puberty, the balance changes and children (or young adults, if you prefer) become more specialist in running as their dominant muscle type develops, i.e. fast twitch or slow twitch (see box for definitions). It is interesting to note that while training has some effect on the balance of fast twitch/slow twitch muscle, it seems that the biggest factor is genetic. According to some studies, and to what we have heard from sport scientists we work with, the genetic factor can be as much as 75 per cent in establishing which muscle type dominates and determines athletes' strengths of pace or endurance, although we have also seen how lifestyle factors and influences in training can reduce or increase this dominance.

MUSCLE TYPES

- **Slow twitch (Type I)** – Working with aerobic energy, Type I muscle fibres twitch between 10 and 30 times a second, and are able to keep working for longer than fast twitch fibres. Players with better developed slow twitch response will typically be able to run further, and for longer. Midfielders often fall into this category, running from one end of the pitch to another for 90 minutes while still being able to play good football.
- **Fast twitch (Type IIa)** – Type IIa fibres are in a sense the intermediate type, drawing on both aerobic and anaerobic energy to twitch 30–70 times a second and provide quick burst of energy.
- **Fast twitch (Type IIb)** – Type IIb fibres, though they twitch at the same frequency as Type IIa fibres, work from anaerobic energy sources alone. This means that they provide a boost of energy to Type IIa fibres and allow explosive sprinting. The quick sprinting of pacy forward players typifies this kind of muscle activity.

Temperature control and fluid loss

Children rely much more on radiation and convection to dissipate heat from the skin, rather than perspiration, and the sweating that they do is more likely to be from the head and not the rest of the body. The body's sweating process only becomes fully functional around puberty. Children have higher body and skin temperatures, and the cooling process of sweating is started at a higher core temperature than in adults, as shown in the three examples in Table 2.2:

TABLE 2.2	RATES OF PERSPIRATION
Age	Rate of perspiration during exercise (square m/hour)
9–10 years	350 ml
12–13 years	400–500 ml
18 years +	600–800 ml

Due to high breathing rate and less body fluid it is easy for children to become dehydrated in warm conditions. Give children a break every 20 minutes in warm conditions for them to rehydrate. (For more on hydration, see page 173 in Chapter 4.)

In cold environments children are more vulnerable to hypothermia than adults. This is due to lower body fat levels, and the fact that children have less blood, with their blood vessels being close to the skin.

Flexibility, or 'suppleness'

Often defined as the range of movement around the joint or series of joints, we always impress on our players that maintaining flexibility is a case of 'use it or lose it'. We start to lose flexibility at a very early age, maybe as early as seven years old for boys, so the chances are that the younger your players, the better their range of movement will be. This is covered in detail in the section on suppleness as one of the four 'S's' on pages 49–58.

Designing a conditioning programme for young players

Essentially, as long as you bear the points in this chapter in mind there is no difference between developing a programme for young players and an adult team. Simply follow the guidance in Chapter 5. The box below summarises a few points from this chapter, up to now, before we move on from the 'Do's' and 'Don'ts' to talk about the benefits of a conditioning programme.

BASIC QUESTIONS TO BE ASKED BEFORE INTRODUCING A CONDITIONING TRAINING PROGRAMME

If the answer to any of these questions is 'no', you need to plan some more and rethink your approach:

- Is the player ready to participate physically in a conditioning programme?
- Is the player ready to participate psychologically and emotionally?
- Does the coach/conditioner understand the correct techniques and safety issues?
- Is the programme planned with a long-term goal?
- Have you made sure that you are aware of any relevant physical injury history?

Benefits of a conditioning programme

Before you develop a conditioning programme, you must be clear what it and each of its component elements is intended to achieve. The following list should help give you some focus.

Your programme aims to improve:
- cardiovascular performance
- muscular strength and endurance
- strength and balance around the joints
- chance of stimulating bone growth (research has shown that the more stimulation (exercise) you have, the more bone growth is promoted)
- motor skills and coordination
- techniques, posture and core stability
- flexibility/suppleness and to maintain a good level
- overall sporting performance
- physical self-esteem and body image (confidence in physical appearance)
- quality of life and wellbeing
- protection against sporting injuries.

THE FOUR 'S'S

The following four sections contain the key information and conditioning drills we have developed over the years for Strength, Suppleness, Stamina and Speed.

If you intend to use the drills with young players, be sure to note which ones are suitable. The information panel clearly highlights which drills can be used by pre-pubescent and post-pubescent players. Drills suitable for younger players will have information on how they can be adapted.

Strength

When to begin strength work, like all the other 'S's, has long been debated – all young players (from the age of about nine) can undertake at least a minimum-level strength programme, if only to improve self-belief and confidence, and to educate them for the future. Strength is not a priority in the overall picture of kids playing football or doing fitness, but we must make the kids aware of the benefits of strength and teach them good habits. Some players may perceive it as a punishment, but you need to impress on them that it is a basic foundation, and you can teach this in a safe, age-related, fun way. The old saying, 'A little and often' is the guideline – even just a few minutes in every session with the younger players.

TEN GOLDEN RULES FOR STRENGTH WORK

1. Always think 'safety first' – Is the location safe? Is clothing appropriate for the activity and the conditions? Is the drill/exercise relevant for particular individuals?
2. Ensure all groups and sessions are supervised – the greater the coach-to-child ratio the better.
3. Think 'a little and often' – a few minutes every session or alternate session, depending on age.
4. Ensure quality instead of quantity.
5. Never forget basic teaching sequence – **Explain** the drill, **demonstrate** the technique, make the players **practise** the drill and then **correct** if necessary.
6. Keep 'key coaching points' short and simple, as players find a lot of new information hard to process all at once.
7. Ensure good technique for lifting and lowering any weights, i.e. 'straight back and bent knees'.
8. Be aware that most strength exercises require balance and coordination to be effective.
9. Always use appropriately weighted medicine balls (see Table 2.3 below).
10 Always encourage the kids, no matter how well they are performing the drill.

Why do strength work with kids?
- Promotes self confidence and belief
- Improves motor skills
- Improves core stability and balance.

TABLE 2.3	APPROXIMATE MEDICINE BALL WEIGHT GUIDELINES
AGE	WEIGHT
9–11 years	2–4 kg
12–13 years	4–6 kg
14–15 years	6–8 kg
16 years +	7–9 kg

Note: These are broad guidelines – as with so many other factors of conditioning we have discussed, it is down to your careful judgement as to which weights you feel it appropriate to use with different age groups.

Strength drills

Below are 10 strength drills for you to incorporate into your programme and adapt where necessary.

> I was very lucky to be naturally fit and quick, but I now realise playing soccer as a kid made me even faster, stronger and fitter.
>
> *David Unsworth, former England International*

1.

Strength Drill
Push 'N' Pull

Age group:	9 years +
Purpose:	Develop upper body strength work with medicine ball
Equipment:	Appropriate weighted medicine balls (suggest players share)
Duration:	2–3 mins each player
Space:	N/A
Number of participants:	N/A – 1 medicine ball between 3 or 4 players

Ensure the players get a feel of the medicine ball before starting the exercise.

If balance, core stability and coordination need improvement, players should place one foot in front of the other.

Players stand upright with the ball in both hands in front of them, arms bent, and then:

1. push out horizontally forwards
2. pull back in
3. raise arms above the head and push up vertically
4. lower arms back down.

KEY COACHING POINTS

1. The emphasis is on strong core and back (upright posture).
2. Do not lock out elbows when carrying out stages 1–4.
3. Remind the kids not to forget to breathe!

2.

Strength Drill
Drop And Throw

Age group:	9 years +
Purpose:	Upper body dynamic strength work with medicine ball
Equipment:	Appropriately weighted medicine balls (suggest players share)
Duration:	2–3 mins each player
Space:	N/A
Number of participants:	Ideally an even number, in pairs

This drill develops upper body strength and power in a safe way. Ensure the players get a feel of the medicine ball before starting the exercise.

1. Player standing drops the ball into partner's hands.
2. Partner catches, brings ball to chest, then with explosive movement throws ball back to other player.
3. Repeat.

KEY COACHING POINTS

1. Make sure both partners are ready before starting.
2. Player on the floor ensures feet and head never leave the floor.
3. Receiver always aims for the chest.
4. Player on the floor has his knees bent as shown and gently pushes his back onto the floor.

3.

Strength Drill
Chest Throws

Age group:	9 years +
Purpose:	Upper body strength work with medicine ball
Equipment:	Appropriately weighted medicine balls (suggest players share)
Duration:	2–3 mins each player
Space:	N/A
Number of participants:	Ideally an even number, in pairs

Ensure the players get a feel of the medicine ball before starting the exercise. Players stand 2–5 metres apart. First player throws the ball to partner's chest, partner catches it and throws it back to the first player's chest. Players are always slightly leaning forwards.

KEY COACHING POINTS

1. Do not lock out elbows when carrying out this exercise – the emphasis is on strong core and back (upright posture).
2. Always aim at chest.
3. If balance, core and coordination need improvement, players should place one foot in front of the other.

4.

Strength Drill
Kneeling Chest Throw

Age group:	9 years +
Purpose:	Upper body strength work with medicine ball
Equipment:	Appropriately weighted medicine balls (suggest players share)
Duration:	2–3 mins each player
Space:	N/A
Number of participants:	Ideally an even number, in pairs

Ensure the players get a feel of the medicine ball before starting the exercise. Players stand 2–4 metres apart. First player throws the ball to partner's chest, partner catches it and throws it back.

KEY COACHING POINTS

1. Do not lock out elbows when carrying out this exercise – the emphasis is on strong core and back, with upright posture.
2. If balance, core and coordination need improvement, players should kneel on one leg only.
3. Players are always slightly leaning forwards.

5.

Strength Drill
Press-Up – Three
Adaptations

Age group:	9 years +
Purpose:	All round strength work
Equipment:	None
Duration:	2–3 mins each player
Space:	N/A
Number of participants:	N/A

Box press-up ① ②

Knee press-up ① ②

Full press-up ① ②

Age guidelines for press-ups:

9–11 years	Box press-ups
12–13 years	Knee press-ups
14–16 years	Full press-ups

BOX PRESS-UPS

1. Starting position as shown.
2. Back should always be straight, not arched.
3. When arms are bent at 90 degrees, push up again.

KNEE PRESS-UPS

1. Starting position as shown. Weight of lower body is just above the knees & not on the knees.
2. Back should always be straight, not arched.
3. Lower body towards the ground – when arms are bent at 90 degrees, push up. Body must always be in line, i.e. head, neck, spine and buttocks (as shown in the diagram).

FULL PRESS-UPS

1. Starting position as shown.
2. Keep body straight, legs slightly apart, hands more than shoulder-width apart.
3. Back is always flat, not arched.
4. Slowly lower body towards the ground – when arms are bent at 90 degrees, push up again. Body must always be in line.

KEY COACHING POINTS

1. If you have any doubts about ability, let the players choose which exercise they feel is appropriate for themselves.
2. Emphasis is on a straight and strong back.
3. Arm action is from straight elbow (just before lock) to 90 degrees.

6.

Strength Drill
Lunges

Age group:	9 years +
Purpose:	Strength work working lower body and legs
Equipment:	Ball
Duration:	2–3 mins each player
Space:	N/A
Number of participants:	Ideally an even number, in pairs

1. Starting position as shown in diagram (1).
2. Keep feet hip-width apart.
3. Slowly take a semi-large step and bend both knees as shown in diagram (2).
4. Hold for a split second in that position.
5. Push back up and return to starting position.
6. Repeat by working opposite leg.

KEY COACHING POINTS

1. Do not let leading leg knee go beyond toes.
2. Do not lose balance when taking semi-large step or overstretch (reduce length of step if necessary).
3. Keep back straight, with upright posture from hip upwards.
4. Bend knees to approx 90 degrees.

7.

Strength Drill Lunges

Age group: 9 years +
Purpose: Strength work for legs
Equipment: Ball
Duration: 2–3 mins
Space: N/A
Number of
participants: Ideally an even number, in pairs

1. Starting position as shown in diagram.
2. Keep feet slightly more than shoulder width apart.
3. Slowly bend knees 90 degrees as shown in diagram.
4. Return to starting position slowly.

KEY COACHING POINTS

1. Keep back straight/flat at all times.
2. Do not bend knees more than 90 degrees.
3. In second part of drill, ensure knees do not go beyond toes.
4. Do not make any jerky or sudden movements.

8.

Strength Drill
Basic Sit-Ups

Age group:	9 years +
Purpose:	Strength work for the stomach
Equipment:	N/A
Duration:	2–3 mins
Space:	N/A
Number of participants:	Ideally an even number, in pairs

①  ②

1. Starting position as shown in diagram, with knees bent and feet on floor.
2. Partner gently supports player's feet.
3. Action is a small movement as shown in diagram, with hands sliding up to the knees.
4. Upper back should curl off the floor.
5. Slowly return to starting position.

KEY COACHING POINTS

1. Should be a small, slow and smooth movement with no jerking.
2. Partner gently supports leg.
3. Remind players not to forget to breathe!

9.

Strength Drill
Dorsi Raisers

Age group:	9 years +
Purpose:	Strength work for the lower back
Equipment:	N/A
Duration:	2–3 mins
Space:	N/A
Number of participants:	Ideally an even number, in pairs

1. Starting position as shown on diagram, lying face down, toes touching floor and hands on temples.
2. Slowly raise upper body as shown in diagram.
3. Head-to-floor angle should only be 15 degrees.
4. Slowly lower the upper body to floor again.

KEY COACHING POINTS

1. Feet must always stay in contact with floor.
2. Back should never hyperextend beyond 15 per cent angle.
3. Slow and deliberate movements, not quick and no jerking action.
4. Remind players not to forget to breathe!

10.

Strength Drill
Burpees

Age group:	9 years +
Purpose:	Strength work for the upper and lower body
Equipment:	N/A
Duration:	2–3 mins
Space:	N/A
Number of participants:	Ideally an even number, in pairs

1. Start in standing upright position.
2. Feet are slightly wider than shoulder-width apart.
3. Bend down (using knees).
4. Immediately push out legs (press-up position).
5. Return to position 2 and then 1, and carry out a small two-footed jump, so feet only just leave the floor.

KEY COACHING POINTS

1. Slow, controlled but dynamic continuous movement.
2. Keep back as flat as possible.
3. Try to keep head pointing in front.
4. Focus on keeping your balance.

Suppleness

A good range of flexibility is a very important factor of a healthy lifestyle. Like all the other physical main building blocks for kids, it's about education, good habits and thinking about the future, and not just about doing the exercise.

Lack of stretching causes lack of suppleness, which in turn will cause restricted movement, and that can lead to frustration and a lack of enjoyment. Some research suggests that you should be stretching at a very early age, as young as six or seven, although flexibility can be developed at any age, subject to appropriate training and supervision. Research has also shown that if you don't continue to stretch you will lose flexibility very quickly.

Generally speaking, children are at their most flexible between the ages of seven and 14, subject to the child's individual growth spurt (see pages 26 and 27 for guidelines on the growth spurt).

Another factor of the growth spurt is that bones, muscles and joints grow at different rates. Consequently, this can cause tightening of muscles, and hence makes children more vulnerable to injury during their growth spurt.

Dynamic or static stretches?

Both forms of stretches are excellent, but our preference is for dynamic stretching, 10 examples of which we have included on pages 49–58.

Dynamic stretching is the more realistic form, as it reflects the way we play football, which is a dynamic game. For an overview of the definition of a static or dynamic stretch, see Matt Byard's advice in Appendix 4 on page 206.

If these drills whet your whistle and you want to expand and adapt the stretching drills you include in your programme, we can suggest other dynamic movements that stretch and increase your range of movement, such as:

- Butt kicks
- High knees
- High-knee butt kicks
- Ankle flips
- Knee swings
- Side swings.

If you are interested in developing these stretches we recommend *Dynamic Flexibility* by Alan Pearson, published by A&C Black (see bibliography for publishing details).

NINE GOLDEN RULES FOR SUPPLENESS

1. Use dynamic stretching before exercise as the most effective way of avoiding injury.
2. Educate the children on why you are doing the stretches.
3. Choose a combination of any five of the stretches that follow.
4. Carry out each stretch for approx 20 secs.
5. Carry out all movements in a controlled fashion.
6. All stretches are continuous flowing movements.
7. Do not force any of the movements.
8. Ensure the kids feel the stretches in the right place and are performing them correctly.
9. Remember that the other benefits of this form of stretching include improved balance and coordination.

Work on your weakness but keep on strengthening your strengths. Play football with a smile.

Darren Currie, over 400 games in the Championship

1.

Suppleness Drill
Funny Walk

Age group: All age groups
Purpose: To stretch the hamstring
Equipment: N/A
Duration: Approx. 20 secs each stretch
Space: Any clear area
Number of
participants: N/A

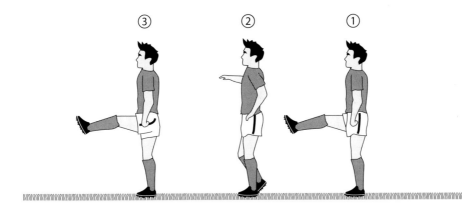

1. Walking in a straight line, raise one leg slowly.
2. Lower leg slowly.
3. Take a few steps and raise opposite leg slowly.
4. Lower leg slowly.
5. Repeat several times.

KEY COACHING POINTS

1. Straight posture is important.
2. All movements must be controlled.
3. Do not 'lock out' knees when at full extension.
4. Movement should be generated from the hip.

2.

Suppleness Drill
Floor Touches

Age group:	All age groups
Purpose:	To stretch quads
Equipment:	N/A
Duration:	Approx. 20 secs each stretch
Space:	Any clear area
Number of participants:	N/A

1. Walking in a straight line, bend down and gently grip the ankle (1).
2. Lean forwards, taking the leg back, and try to touch the floor with the opposite hand (2).
3. Release leg, stand up straight, take a few steps (3), and repeat on opposite leg.
4. Repeat twice more.

KEY COACHING POINTS

1. Ensure players do not lose their balance.
2. All movements must be controlled.
3. Do not pull on the ankle.

3.

Suppleness Drill
Tiptoe Reaches

Age group:	All age groups
Purpose:	To stretch upper calf muscle and upper body
Equipment:	N/A
Duration:	Approx. 20 secs
Space:	Any clear area
Number of participants:	N/A

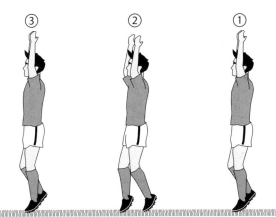

1. Walking on your toes, raise your arms above your head (1).
2. Continue walking on your toes for several steps (2/3).

KEY COACHING POINTS

1. Straight posture is important.
2. Steps should be small and controlled.
3. Check that the players feel a stretch from toes to fingertips.

4.

Suppleness Drill
Walk to Heel

Age group:	All age groups
Purpose:	To stretch lower calf muscles and upper body
Equipment:	N/A
Duration:	Approx. 20 seconds
Space:	Any clear area
Number of participants:	N/A

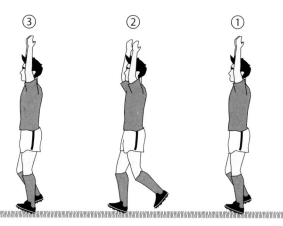

1. Walking on your heels, raise arms above your head.
2. Continue walking on your heels for several steps.

KEY COACHING POINTS

1. Toes should be pointing upwards as much as possible.
2. Do not overstrain.
3. Straight posture is important.
4. Steps should be small and controlled.
5. Check that the players feel a stretch from toes to fingertips.

5.

Suppleness Drill
Knee to Chest

Age group:	All age groups
Purpose:	To stretch gluteal (buttock) muscles
Equipment:	N/A
Duration:	Approx. 20 seconds
Space:	Any clear area
Number of participants:	N/A

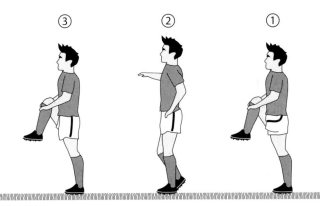

1. Walking in a straight line, slowly raise one of your legs and grab with your hands, squeezing the top of your thigh to your chest (1).
2. Release slowly and take a few steps (2).
3. Repeat again on opposite leg (3).
4. Repeat twice more on each leg.

KEY COACHING POINTS
1. Players should 'stand tall' with straight posture.
2. Thigh squeeze with arms should be performed gently.
3. Ensure balance is good.
4. Keep posture upright.

6.

Suppleness Drill
Walk and Lunge

Age group:	All age groups
Purpose:	To stretch hip flexors and quads
Equipment:	N/A
Duration:	Approx. 20 seconds
Space:	Any clear area
Number of participants:	N/A

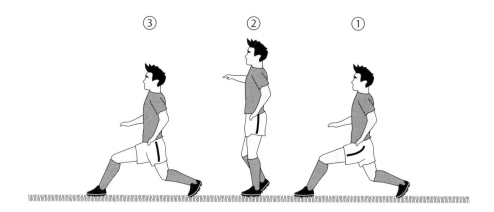

1. Walking in a straight line, slowly carry out a controlled lunge by bending your knees (1).
2. Slowly push yourself up, take a few steps (2) and repeat, but changing lead foot (3).
3. Repeat whole drill several times.

KEY COACHING POINTS

1. When both knees are bent and you are in the lunge position, looking up will increase the stretch.
2. Legs are working slightly more than shoulder-width apart.
3. From the hip above, the posture is upright.
4. Do not bend the knees more than 90 degrees.

7.

Suppleness Drill
The Sumo

Age group:	All age groups
Purpose:	To stretch the inner thighs
Equipment:	N/A
Duration:	Approx. 20 seconds
Space:	Any clear area
Number of participants:	N/A

1. Walking in a straight line, take a lateral wide step and slowly bend your knees (1).
2. Place your elbows inside your thighs and for a split second gently push your thighs with your elbows out.
3. Gently push yourself up and take a few steps (2).
4. Repeat several times.

KEY COACHING POINTS
1. Keep back straight at all times.
2. Keep good balance.
3. Keep thighs horizontal to floor when stretching.
4. Do not bend knees more than 90 degrees.

8.

Suppleness Drill Over the Gate

Age group:	All age groups
Purpose:	To increase range of movement and stretch around the hips and inner thighs
Equipment:	N/A
Duration:	Approx. 20 seconds
Space:	Any clear area
Number of participants:	N/A

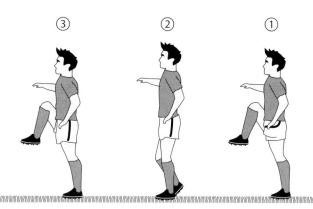

1. Walking in a straight line, pretend you are going over a gate or hurdle.
2. Take a few steps and repeat with opposite leg.
3. Do this several times.

KEY COACHING POINTS

1. All movements should be controlled.
2. Use arms for balance.
3. Use smooth movements with no jerking.
4. Use as high a knee movement as possible.

9.

Suppleness Drill
Elbow and Knee Kisses

Age group:	All age groups
Purpose:	To increase range of movement around the hips and back
Equipment:	N/A
Duration:	Approx. 20 secs
Space:	Any clear area
Number of participants:	N/A

1. Walking in a straight line, raise your right leg and move it slightly across your body.
2. At the same time lower your left elbow at an angle across your body so elbow and knee touch each other.
3. Take a few steps and repeat the opposite way.
4. Repeat whole drill several times.

KEY COACHING POINTS

1. Keep good balance.
2. Do not force motion.
3. Elbow and opposite knee must work in conjunction.
4. Use other arm for balance.
5. Maintain as upright a posture as possible, and try not to crouch.

10.

Suppleness Drill
Wait on Hand and Foot

Age group:	All age groups
Purpose:	To increase range of movement around the hips, legs and back
Equipment:	N/A
Duration:	Approx. 20 secs
Space:	Any clear area
Number of participants:	N/A

1. Walking in a straight line, raise your right leg and foot and move them slightly across your body.
2. At the same time, lower your left hand at an angle across your body so hand and foot touch each other.
3. Take a few steps and repeat the opposite way.
4. Repeat whole drill several times.

KEY COACHING POINTS

1. Keep good balance.
2. Do not force motion.
3. Elbow and opposite knee must work in conjunction.
4. Use other arm for balance.
5. Maintain as upright a posture as possible, and try not to crouch.
6. Do not lock knees.

Stamina

Stamina is sometimes described as 'endurance'. To a certain extent, just playing and practising football will improve a young player's stamina, as long as the sessions are well planned and structured with plenty of breaks.

However, there is a place for specific stamina drills at the right time and place when players get older, and certainly after growth spurt. We would have them doing some of the following drills for three main reasons:

- to help them develop mental strength and attitude
- to get them used to harder physical work in a controlled environment
- to improve their stamina in a different and varied way.

By getting them to do these drills, you are basically looking at the 'bigger picture' of what football can offer.

We have noticed over the last 10 years that kids are not only becoming less fit, as previously mentioned in the introduction they also seem to be getting 'softer'! This is not their fault to a large extent, but despite our repeated message that you must not harm children's development, we would ask you to look at what football has to offer if you think 'out of the box', i.e. the benefits of playing football that can introduce some hardiness to young players as they develop skills and a knowledge of the game.

As you will see, all the following drills are done with a ball. Also remind the players that these drills are very similar to what the professional players use to train. In our experience, this is always a great motivator and benchmark.

PERCEIVED EXERTION

'Perceived exertion' is a simple but effective way to measure a player's effort, as long as that player is honest! An honest appraisal is important for this to work, so always ask a cross-section of the kids you trust to give you a straight answer. Follow the table below as a simple guideline to responses, with the number being the 'rate of perceived exertion' (RPE). All the players have to do is judge how hard they are working, after each set they have performed. These are the kind of responses you are looking for:

1. 'Easy' – literally, like 'a walk in the park'.
2. 'No problems – feels very comfortable.'
3. 'It's like playing outside in a playground or on the beach.'

4. 'It's OK – not easy but not hard either.'
5. 'It's getting harder. I am getting hotter.'
6. 'This is hard work. I am feeling it.'
7. '. . .' – silence from the players because they are working so hard.
8. 'It's tough . . . It's very hard work.'
9. Players might start dropping out.
10 'This is the hardest exercise I have done! I don't think I can do any more.'

Remember that every young player has a different level of fitness, so always go for the average ratings, but keep an eye on the kids who are struggling. You can also dictate the intensity of every session by telling the kids to work faster or more slowly.

TEN GOLDEN RULES FOR STAMINA

1. Educate the players on why they are doing these drills.
2. Emphasis is always on quality with the ball.
3. Get the players to work at a perceived exertion of 7 to 8 (see above box for a description of 'rates of perceived exertion').
4. Pay special attention to when the players get tired, as that is when mistakes occur with the ball.
5. Give the players plenty of rest breaks.
6. Ensure all the players have plenty to drink (see Chapter 4)
7. Get the players to stretch between sets (see sample session plans on pages 184–6 for specifics).
8. Sets should last 2–3 mins, subject to players' needs and development.
9. Give plenty of encouragement during the drills.
10. Congratulate players on their efforts, regardless of their ability or level of achievement.

1.

Stamina Drill
Dribbling with a Ball

Age group: Usually after growth spurt
Purpose: Interval training with a ball
Equipment: One ball and several cones per group
Duration: Between 10–15 mins (subject to purpose and age group)
Space: 30-/40-metre strips per group of three
Number of
participants: Groups of three

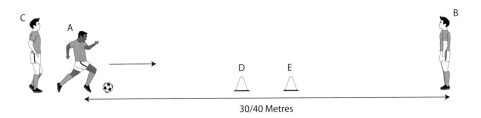

30/40 Metres

1. Players are set up as shown in diagram.
2. 'A' dribbles the ball to 'B' ('A' stays where 'B' was).
3. 'B' then dribbles the ball to 'C' ('B' stays where 'C' was).
4. 'C' then dribbles the ball to 'A' ('C' stays where 'A' was).
5. 'A' goes again.
6. Continue this for approx. 2 or 3 mins.
7. Rest for one minute, and repeat several times.

Note: To make this drill more interesting and fun, the kids have to do a trick or skill of your choice between the cones marked 'D' and 'E'.

KEY COACHING POINTS

1. Encourage the players to be comfortable using the ball.
2. Players need to maintain concentration, even when they are without the ball and waiting.
3. Insist on a good tempo (subject to perceived exertion levels).
4. When kids hand over the ball, encourage good communication between the players.

2.

Stamina Drill
Pass and Run

Age group:	10 or 11 +
Purpose:	Passing drill with a ball
Equipment:	One ball and 4 cones between groups
Duration:	10–15 mins (subject to age)
Space:	Area 20–25 m length
Number of participants:	Groups of five

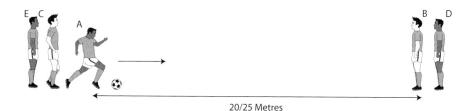

20/25 Metres

1. Players are set up as shown in diagram, about 20–25 metres apart.
2. 'A' passes the ball to 'B' ('A' runs where 'B' was).
3. 'B' then passes the ball to 'C' ('B' runs where 'C' was).
4. 'C' then passes the ball to 'D' ('C' runs where 'D' was).
5. 'D' passes the ball to 'E' ('D' runs where 'E' was).
6. 'E' passes the ball back to 'A' ('E' runs to where 'A' was).
7. Continue this for approximately 3 minutes.
8. Rest for one minute.
9. Repeat whole drill several times.

KEY COACHING POINTS

1. Players have more chance to rest during this drill, so you can work longer in each set.
2. When the players pass the ball, you are looking for a change of pace for the run.
3. Players can have two or three touches to control and pass.
4. Encourage the players to be comfortable with the ball.
5. Players need to maintain concentration, even when they are without the ball and waiting.

3.

Stamina Drill
Beat the Runner

Age group:	10 or 11 years +
Purpose:	Fun/competitive passing and running drill
Equipment:	1 ball and 4 cones per group
Duration:	10–15 mins (subject to age group)
Space:	10 x 10 m square
Number of participants:	4 players per group

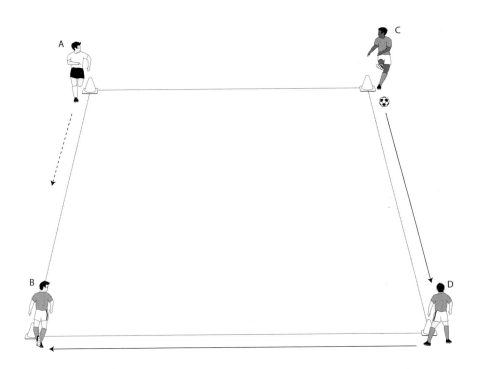

This is a race that should test how the players cope with performing under pressure, but in a fun way.

1. Players are set up as shown in the diagram.
2. 'A' runs around the square twice, as quickly as possible.
3. At the same time 'C', 'D' and 'B' have to pass the ball around the two sides, 'CD' and 'DB', six times.
4. Repeat with other players.
5. Each player should do this 4–8 times.

KEY COACHING POINTS

1. Encourage the players to be comfortable with the ball.
2. Players need to maintain concentration, even when they are without the ball and waiting.
3. Players with the ball have to take one or two touches, and have to count aloud when they complete one sequence, to make it competitive and fun.

'If you don't enjoy training or playing, you will never achieve anything, so go out there and enjoy it.'

Shane Supple, Republic of Ireland Youth International

4.

Stamina Drill
Mini Game

Age group:	Growth spurt onwards
Purpose:	Small-sided game
Equipment:	Two small goals, plenty of balls, cones
Duration:	10–15 mins (subject to age group)
Space:	30 x 20 m
Number of participants:	8 players per game (4-a-side), 8 players resting

1. Players compete as if in a real match situation.
2. All spare players stand around the outside waiting their turn.
3. Keep plenty of spare balls in the goals to keep the game moving if a ball goes out.
4. Play for 24 minutes, subject to age.
5. There should ideally be a 1:1 ratio of work to rest, e.g. work 2 minutes, then rest 2 minutes on the outside of the pitch while other groups play.

KEY COACHING POINTS
1. Simply let them play.
2. Maintain a high tempo.
3. Give plenty of encouragement.
4. Players are not allowed to stand still, must always be on the move even when not in possession.
5. Watch out for lazy players!

5.

Stamina Drill
Dribble, Pass and Run

Age group:	10 or 11 years +
Purpose:	Dribble and pass drill
Equipment:	1 ball and 6 cones per group
Duration:	10–15 mins (subject to age group)
Space:	30 x 5 m square
Number of participants:	3 per group

1. 'A' dribbles to mid line, then passes to 'C' ('A' then sprints to 'C' and waits).
2. 'C' dribbles to mid line, then passes to 'B' ('C' then sprints to 'B' and waits).
3. 'B' dribbles to mid line, then passes to 'A' ('B' then sprints to 'A' and waits).
4. Continue this for approximately 2 minutes.
5. Rest for one minute.
6. Repeat whole drill several times.

KEY COACHING POINTS

1. Players have more rest during this drill, so you can work longer in each set.
2. When the players pass the ball, you are looking for a change of pace for the run.
3. Players can have 2 or 3 touches to control and pass.
4. Encourage the players to be comfortable with the ball.
5. Players need to maintain concentration, even when they are without the ball and waiting.

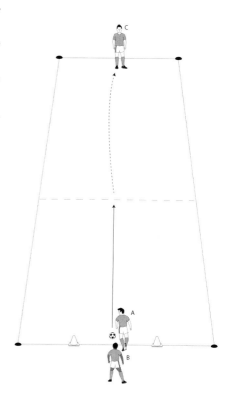

6.

Stamina Drill
Screwball Scramble

Age group:	10 or 11 years +
Purpose:	Multidirectional aerobic training with a ball using various equipment
Equipment:	Ladders, poles, cones, hurdles and balls
Duration:	2–3 min efforts; total 20 mins (subject to age group)
Space:	Approx. 10m width, 35m length
Number of participants:	Approx. 5/6 players per line

We named this after the children's game in which a silver ball-bearing is guided through all sorts of obstacles. Except that in this drill the kids are the silver ball!

Possible sections of the course are:

1. Quick feet through ladders
2. Shimmy in and out of poles
3. Lateral work running in between cones
4. Bounding over 6/8 inch hurdles
5. Three passes against bench – right-footed, left-footed, right-footed.

Player jogs back to the beginning and joins back of line of other players. Continue for 2 to 3 minutes.

KEY COACHING POINTS
1. Gap between players starting the drill is 2–3 seconds.
2. Head should always be up, looking ahead.
3. Encourage the players to use quick feet at the appropriate parts of drill.
4. Encourage quality with the ball.
5. Change patterns with each repetition.
6. Feel free to add your own variations that perform same job as the above.

7.

Stamina Drill
X-Box Sprints

Age group:	Growth spurt onwards
Purpose:	Multi-directional speed endurance, with a ball
Equipment:	4 cones, 1 ball
Duration:	2 players working, approx. 10 mins
Space:	10 x 10 m square
Number of participants:	2 per square, maximum subject to equipment available

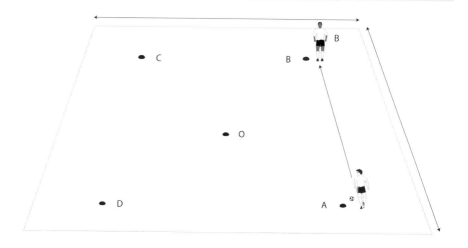

Two players together, one working and the other receiving the pass.

1. Player at A passes ball to partner at B.
2. Player at A sprints A-O-A-B (partner at B moves to C).
3. Player passes ball to partner at C.
4. Player at B sprints B-O-B-C (partner at C moves to D).
5. Player passes ball to partner at D.
6. Player at C sprints C-O-C-D (partner at D moves to A).
7. Player passes ball to partner at A.
8. Player at D sprints D-O-D-A.
9. 90 secs active rest (e.g. walking/jogging/simple passes between the two partners).

10. Player at A then passes to partner at D, reversing the route around the box, so A-O-A-D, then D-O-D-C, etc.
11. First player does anti-clockwise circuit/90 secs active rest/clockwise circuit sequence 2–5 times (subject to age group).
12. Partners swap over and repeat the whole of the above drill in opposite roles.

KEY COACHING POINTS

1. Encourage quality with the ball.
2. Focus on turns and dropping shoulder on inside.
3. There should be a smooth transition from passing to running, turning to passing again.

8.

Stamina Drill
Fetch my Ball!

Age group: Growth spurt onwards
Purpose: Aerobic interval training with ball and turns
Equipment: 8 cones per pair working, 1 ball per player
Duration: 10–15 mins
Space: Football pitch
Number of
participants: Even number, in pairs, maximum number subject to
equipment and space available

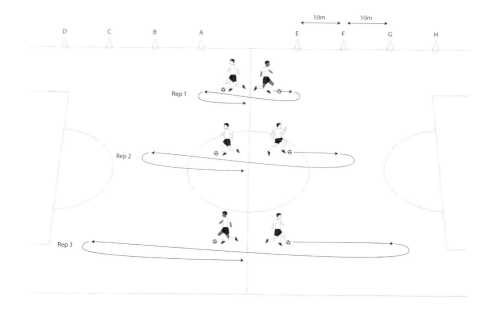

Each player starts with a ball on the halfway line.

Rep 1 – Player runs with ball to 'A' and leaves ball at 'A'. Partner working in the opposite half therefore runs with ball to 'E' and leaves ball at 'E'. Both players then turn, run 20 metres past each other, pick up each other's ball, turn and run back with ball to starting position. Players rest for 10–15 seconds.

Rep 2 – As above, but to B and F respectively.

Rep 3 – As above, but to C and G respectively.

Rep 4 – As above, but to D and H respectively.

Work for approx 3 minutes. Follow with 2 minutes of active rest, which should be 'head tennis' in pairs.

KEY COACHING POINTS

1. Emphasis should be on quality with ball, especially when tired.
2. Focus on change of pace from dribbling phase to running phase (latter is always quicker in this drill).
3. There are many adaptations to this drill, so use your imagination.

9.

Stamina Drill
Cone Relays

Age group:	After growth spurt
Purpose:	Aerobic conditioning with a ball
Equipment:	1 ball and 6 cones per pair
Duration:	10–15 mins
Space:	Area at least 50 m in length, width variable
Number of participants:	Even number, no limits

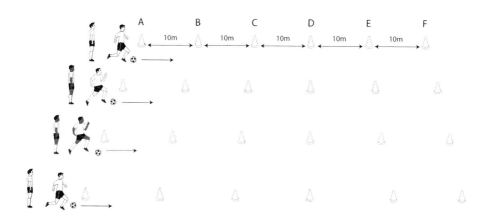

Rep 1 – First player runs with ball to 'B', stops and leaves the ball there. He then turns around, runs to 'A' (without ball), touches cone and runs back to 'B', turns with the ball and passes it to his partner at 'A', who repeats the drill. First player jogs back after passing the ball.

Rep 2 – Once his partner has returned the ball, the first player runs with ball to 'C', stops and leaves it there. He then turns around, runs to 'A' (without ball), touches cone and runs back to 'C', turns with the ball and passes it to his partner at 'A', who repeats the drill. First player jogs back after passing the ball.

Rep 3 – As above, but working to D.

Rep 4 – As above, but working to E.

Rep 5 – As above, but working to F.

Once you have reached the end (Rep 5), start again from Rep 1, untill you have completed 2–3 minutes.

KEY COACHING POINTS

1. Focus on change of pace, from dribbling phase to running phase (the latter phase is always quicker in this drill).
2. Emphasis should be on quality with ball, especially when tired.
3. Passing must be accurate, especially over longer distances.
4. Distances between cones can be reduced subject to age and abilities.

10.

Stamina Drill
Pass and Score

Age group: After growth spurt
Purpose: Aerobic conditioning in a small-sided game with multi-goals
Equipment: Plenty of balls, 12–14 poles (or cones) and discs
Duration: 10–15 mins
Space: 30 or 40 m square
Number of
participants: 8, 10, 12, 14 or 16 players

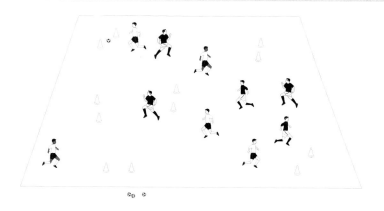

The aim of the game is to score a goal by passing the ball to a team-mate between the poles or cones as shown. Players cannot run through the cones. Play each game for approx. 2–3 minutes. Play about 4–5 games.

KEY COACHING POINTS

1. To play and win these games, players must have good communication with each other.
2. Beware of lazy players!
3. Make sure players are always on the move, looking for the ball and/or space to create openings.
4. Emphasis is on keeping possession of the ball.

Speed

You might reasonably ask why should we do speed work with children when we know that the anaerobic system does not really develop until after puberty (growth spurt). As with so many other aspects, we can work with children on these drills for the following reasons:
- Speed drills instil good training habits (techniques etc.)
- The drills introduce an important building block for other forms of conditioning when kids get older
- It can encourage fast twitch muscle recruitment without any harmful side effects (patterning)
- Speed work is a natural way of introducing interval training, which is better for young players
- Young players enjoy the drills!

All young players have the potential to improve their speed. Although speed is a variable natural component of a player's genetic make-up to a large extent, you can still improve a player's speed if you make this component a part of every drill session and even part of life.

By doing speed drills regularly, ensuring technical correctness, and doing them 'flat out' with plenty of rest breaks for players, you will be making them quicker than they were before, to some degree at least. It is all to do with recruiting those undecided fast twitch fibres!

Stages and phases of speed

As a coach you must have a basic knowledge of the different stages and phases of speed. The following is a very brief outline of these, based on many years' experience.

The stages of sprinting

Speed includes:
- acceleration
- maximum speed phase
- deceleration phase (when you can no longer maintain your top speed).

However, there are other more detailed components to be aware of to improve speed. In our opinion, there are seven physical and mental stages of an average sprint:
1. Mental brightness, alertness and awareness (speed of thought).
2. Anticipation and/or reaction.
3. Golden step (first movement, positive).

4. Upper body awareness/movement.
5. Initial steps (acceleration phase).
6. Technique/running mechanics.
7. Deceleration.

We have learned that if you can improve two or more of these components (be they physical of mental), statistically you will run faster.

Speed of thought

Mental brightness, awareness or alertness – call it what you will – is the first stage of the process and, therefore, the key. Every time you watch a football match on TV, you will hear the commentator lament that a player 'switched off for a second' because his mind was elsewhere and so his body could not follow.

It is a psychological demand, and so is one that is often overlooked on the training ground. There are three elements to mental brightness:

- concentration
- research
- the ability to learn on the pitch.

The first is vital – a player must develop the ability to focus and pay attention to the game from the first whistle to the last. It sounds easy, but, as anyone who has driven for a long period will know, concentration is a tiring business for adults. . . for children it can be especially difficult.

Although not a priority with children, players should also do their homework – where possible – on the team they are playing and the player they are likely to come up against. What are their strengths and weaknesses? Are they slow to recover from sprints? Are they a short team who struggle with the long ball? Do they launch most of their attacks down the left?

Then, with individuals, are they left- or right-footed? Do they have a particular trick they like to use? What is the best way for the player to deal with all these variables?

Then there is the information to process on the day. Does the opponent marking the player have a niggling injury? Is the wind holding the ball up? What is the surface like?

Every single one of these factors must be considered and processed before a player starts his sprint. Learning all this at as young an age as possible can give a player a real advantage in later years. And they say football is not a thinking person's game!

Anticipation and reaction

Speed work in football should be about anticipation – 'Where is my team-mate going to put the ball?' or, 'The opposition is not going to get that ball – can I

CASE STUDY: QUICK THINKING BRINGS SUCCESS

A case in point, perhaps, is that of Teddy Sheringham. Sheringham never had an abundance of raw pace as a younger footballer, but scored goals at the very highest level wherever he played (including a Champions League final with Manchester United). Because Teddy's mental abilities have not faded, he has still been able to perform at a high level and score goals, despite being in his forties.

get to it?' This is the second mental stage and involves processing all the information received in the first stage and coming to a conclusion.

This mental phase makes all the difference and is the root of the phrase, 'You don't need to go fast to be quick'. We have worked with several players who, when doing speed testing, have not recorded particularly good test results. But watching them play and train on numerous occasions, they seem always to get to the ball first, or intercept the ball, or score goals when their marker is much quicker than they are.

The ability to be one step ahead of your opponent psychologically, have a 'footballing brain' or superior reactions will make the difference at any level, especially youth football.

The 'golden step'

This is the first physical stage of the sprint process. The 'golden step' is an American term which basically means that the first step should be a positive movement, i.e. from a standing start – a forward wide step. It begins motion and starts to transfer body weight in the right direction.

Upper body awareness

This is an often underestimated element of sprint work, with many people considering the arms to be the only part of the upper body that are significant in running. The upper body should be like a pendulum, working in synchrony with legs. When you initially start a sprint, you should try to throw your upper body vigorously forwards in the direction of the first step. If you didn't react and work your legs quickly enough, you would end up flat on your face! When turning, you should throw your upper body in the direction you are going, in a controlled fashion – your legs will follow. Use your body weight to assist you and take some of the load off your legs. Get your body used to the patterns as early as possible.

Acceleration phase

One of the key things that you need to do as a conditioning coach is learn lessons from every sport, and athletics is a prime example. Watch how short-distance sprinters come out of the blocks. Look at their initial steps and body movement, how they keep low, take wide steps and sway their body to give them the power and acceleration to start a sprint. Even in football, with walking or rolling starts, we can learn from these track sprint starts.

Technique and running mechanics

Here is a brief overview of the key components in technique and mechanics:

- **Stride frequency** (foot to ground contact) – Known as stride rate, leg speed or leg cycles. This is basically how many steps you take per second.
- **Stride length** – Finding the ideal stride length is an important part of reaching your potential. Understriding or overstriding will affect your speed.
- **Running economy** – This refers to how everything works together and which part of the body must be relaxed while sprinting and not wasting unnecessary energy (e.g. hands, head and upper body).
- **Body movement** – Leading with the upper body helps you change direction, not just working the arms and shoulders.
- **Knee lift** – Generally speaking, this is the amount of force that you exert when your foot hits the ground, the least possible time your foot stays on the floor during a stride and that backlift, what I call the 'butt kick' (foot coming up behind to the gluteals, or buttocks).

One thing to consider with running technique is that, generally, the younger the player, the more influence you can have on them.

Deceleration phase

Speed endurance training will increase the duration that maximum speed can be maintained. Players should also be encouraged to decelerate in a controlled way – not only will this reduce the chance of injury, but it means that the player is poised and balanced, ready to react to the situation. This becomes more important the older the player gets, especially after growth spurt.

TEN GOLDEN RULES FOR SPEED WORK

1. Do speed drills early in the session.
2. Don't do speed work if players are tired.
3. The younger the players, the more enjoyable you should make the session.
4. Most speed work has to be done flat out – encourage players to give 100 per cent.
5. All speed drills should last no more than several seconds only for young players.
6. Make the drills competitive.
7. Encourage all the players – win or lose, quick or slow.
8. Teach one or two key points only for each drill.
9. Remember that the younger the players are, the more influence you will have on their future technique and training habits.
10. Don't be afraid to use your imagination.

1.

Speed Drill
Arm 'n' Leg Hurdles

Age group:	All age groups
Purpose:	To develop basic leg and arm techniques
Equipment:	16 small hurdles
Duration:	5–10 mins
Space:	20 x 10 m strips.
Number of participants:	N/A

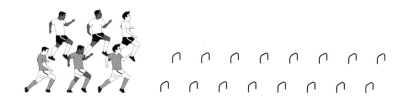

1. Players and equipment set up as shown in diagram – hurdles are approximately 30–60 cm apart.
2. Players work at 2 or 3 second intervals.
3. Working to the left side of the hurdles, right leg only goes over each hurdle with good technique, as fast as possible.
4. Players walk back when they reach the end.
5. Repeat on right-hand side of hurdles with the left leg.
6. Repeat whole drill several times.
7. Players then run through the hurdles with one foot between each hurdle, walking back on each occasion.

KEY COACHING POINTS

1. Emphasis is on knee lift and legs going up and down straight, a pumping arm action, shoulders and hands relaxed, body leaning slightly forwards. Elbows should be fixed at approximately 90 degrees.
2. Encourage the players to get their foot on and off the floor between the hurdles, as fast as possible.
3. Whole body should be kept in line as much as possible.

2. Speed Drill Hot-Foot Hurdles

Age group:	All age groups
Purpose:	To develop speed with agility, using a ball
Equipment:	2 small hurdles and 2 balls per group of 3
Duration:	5–10 mins
Space:	5 x 5 m square
Number of participants:	Groups of 3

1. Players and equipment are set up as shown. Hurdles are approximately 60 cm apart.
2. There are 2 servers, 'A' and 'B', with a ball each.
3. 'A' throws the ball at 'C' who heads it back.
4. 'C' quickly goes over both hurdles laterally.
5. 'B' throws the other ball at 'C' who heads it back.
6. 'C' quickly goes over both hurdles laterally.
7. Do this 10 times and then swap players around.
8. Servers can change service to volleys, ground passes, etc.

KEY COACHING POINTS

1. This has to be a flowing drill with no hesitation, especially by the servers.
2. The servers must deliver the ball just before 'C' reaches the delivery point.
3. Encourage quality with the ball (knocking it back to server's hand without the ball touching the floor).
4. Servers must always stay alert.
5. While carrying out the drill, 'C' is in a slightly crouched position.

3.

Speed Drill
Cone Pinball Runs

Age group:	For all ages
Purpose:	Multidirectional speed agility
Equipment:	Seven traffic cones
Duration:	5–10 mins
Space:	20 x 10 m strips
Number of participants:	N/A

1. Players and equipment are set up as shown – cones should be approximately 3 or 4 metres apart.
2. Players run, one at a time, around all cones as quickly as possible, in numerical order.
3. Players facing 'A' touch the top of all cones as quickly as possible in numerical order.
4. Players facing 'B' go in a forward/backward motion in numerical order.
5. Players facing 'A' start at 1, go forwards to 3, laterally and backwards to 2, forwards to 4, laterally and backwards to 3, forwards to 5, laterally and backwards to 4, forwards to 6, laterally and backwards to 5, forwards to 7, laterally and backwards to 6 and sprint 10 metres.

KEY COACHING POINTS

1. Get the players to adopt a slightly crouched position to assist turning and power.
2. When turning, encourage the players to drop their shoulder and hand (nearest to the cone) on the inside. This will help them work with gravity and therefore turn more quickly.
3. Players should lead slightly with the upper body, especially the head.
4. On turning or changing direction, arms are assisting balance.
5. On turning or changing direction, ensure a smooth transition between movements.

4.

Speed Drill
Coat-Tail Sprints

Age group: For all ages
Purpose: To develop power in a fun way
Equipment: N/A
Duration: 5–10 mins
Space: 20 x 10 m strips
Number of
participants: Even number, in pairs

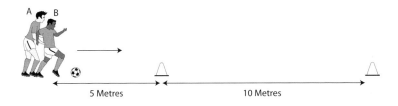

5 Metres   10 Metres

1. Players are set up as shown in diagram.
2. Player 'A' is gently gripping player 'B' by the bottom of his shirt with both hands.
3. When the coach says 'go', player 'A' sprints to the first cone with player 'B' following him, still holding on and creating a constant moderate resistance.
4. When Players 'A' and 'B' reach the cone, 'A' releases the shirt of 'B' – 'B' should feel the acceleration due to no resistance and sprint to the second cone.
5. Repeat this 3 times and then swap over.
6. Both 'A' and 'B' repeat the above, but change the distances of the cones.

KEY COACHING POINTS

1. Before practising this drill, ensure the players' clothing is appropriate and explain to them that they must not pull or tug at their partner's clothing. Their grip should just create a constant resistance.
2. Player 'A' is following the 'golden step' rule at the start of sprint (see page 78).
3. After the initial few steps, there should be a pumping arm action from the shoulder, with shoulders, head and hands relaxed. Body should be leaning slightly forwards. Elbows are fixed at approximately 90 degrees.
4. Encourage 'A' to be aggressive.
5. Also encourage knee lift.

5.

Speed Drill
Your Number's up!

Age group:	All age groups
Purpose:	To develop basic reactions and speed
Equipment:	Approx. 12 cones and 2 poles, subject to numbers
Duration:	5–10 mins
Space:	20 x 10 m strips
Number of participants:	N/A

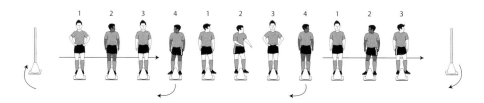

1. Players and equipment set up as shown in diagram.
2. Number the players as shown.
3. You shout out two numbers, e.g. '1' and '4'. Players with those numbers step forwards and sprint around the poles clockwise, each finishing where they started.
4. First player back is the winner.
5. Repeat so that every player gets several goes.

KEY COACHING POINTS

1. All the players are active, e.g. on their toes jogging on the spot.
2. Make it competitive.
3. Encourage turning techniques, i.e. when turning, encourage the players to drop their shoulder and hand (nearest to the pole) on the inside – this is to help them work with gravity and therefore turn more quickly.

6.

Speed Drill
Clockface Sprints

Age group: 9 years +
Purpose: Reaction speed drills. Also being alert and bright
Equipment: 12 cones marked in a circle
Duration: 2–3 minutes or more, depending on age group
Space: Ideally, centre circle
Number of
participants: Ideally in groups of 4

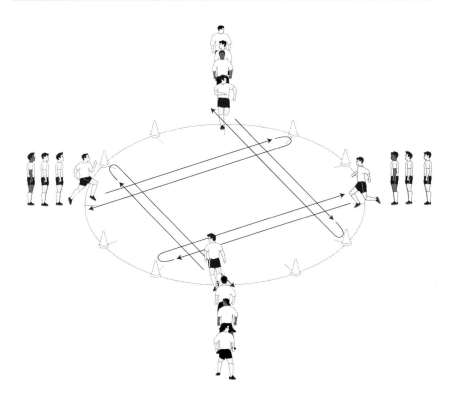

1. Players are marked as 'X'.
2. Circle is effectively marked as a clock face with the 12 cones. Players are all at 12 o'clock in their 4 respective groups – therefore, 6 o'clock is directly opposite, three cones to the left is 3 o'clock, etc.
3. One player goes from each group at a time.
4. Coach shouts a number, e.g. '4 o'clock' – 1 player from each group sprints to 4 o'clock, then sprints back to their starting position at 12 o'clock. Last player back does a fun forfeit of your choice (not 100 press-ups!).

KEY COACHING POINTS

1. Players must always stay alert.
2. Players must touch the cones before returning back.
3. Emphasis is on the golden step rule for starting the sprint.
4. There are many variations to this, including running with a ball.

'Enjoy competing and playing. The key word is enjoyment. Relish playing the game.'
Bryan Klug, first team coach at Ipswich Town FC,
former Academy director and professional player

7.

Speed Drill
Dummy Runs 1

Age group: All age groups
Purpose: Speed work in a competitive relay
Equipment: 1 ball, 3 mannequins (or substitute for poles, etc.) and 1 cone per relay line
Duration: 5 minutes
Space: Depends on number of players
Number of participants: Flexible due to relay format

1. Player 'A' runs with the ball to cone and stops ball dead, then does a figure of '8' around the mannequin and passes the dead ball to 'B'.
2. 'B' must take the ball and himself (stops him cheating!) behind the starting mannequin and repeat drill.
3. Relay finishes when 'E' passes the ball back to 'A' and sprints past the starting mannequin.

KEY COACHING POINTS

1. Emphasis is on speed, but quality with the ball is just as important.
2. When player does figure of 8, emphasis is on dropping the shoulder on the inside turns.
3. There are many variations to this, subject to players' ball skills, your requirements, etc.

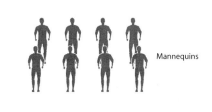

Mannequins

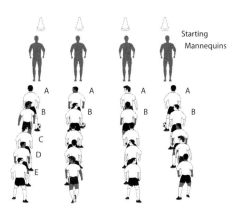

Starting Mannequins

8.

Speed Drill
Between the Sticks Relay

Age group:	All age groups
Purpose:	Competitive sprint drill, relay, anticipation being the key.
Equipment:	4 poles per team
Duration:	5 mins
Space:	Depends on number of players
Number of participants:	Various due to relay format – minimum of 8 (2 teams of 4)

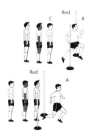 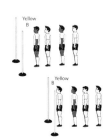

1. Four players line up at each end, approximately 2 metres behind the red or yellow poles, and at a diagonal angle.
2. Player A sprints from starting point through red poles to opposite yellow poles.
3. As 'A' runs through yellow poles, 'B' immediately sprints through them in the opposite direction, having anticipated 'A' passing through and perfectly timed his own run from his own starting point.
4. As 'B' runs through red poles, 'C' immediately sprints through them in the opposite direction, having anticipated 'B' passing through and perfectly timed his own run from his own starting point.
5. Continue until every player has done 2 sprints.

KEY COACHING POINTS
1. Anticipation is the key word in this drill.
2. Timing of passing through the poles is very important.
3. Poles must not be knocked down.
4. Get the players to start the sprint before team-mate goes through the pole.
5. Change distances between poles between sprints.

9.

Speed Drill
Dummy Runs 2

Age group: All age groups
Purpose: To improve players' speed in a competitive environment
Equipment: 2 mannequins and one cone per pair.
Duration: Flexible
Space: Depends on number of players
Number of
participants: Unlimited, subject to equipment and available space

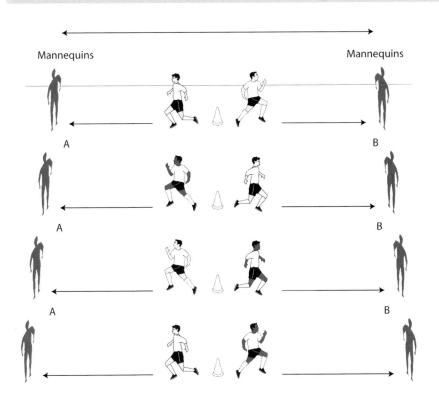

1. Players start and finish at their cones – starting position is actually touching the cone. On the word go, 1 player sprints to mannequin 'A', the other to mannequin 'B'.
2. Both players touch mannequins and sprint past cones to finish.

KEY COACHING POINTS

1. Try to work to a minimum of 1:4 ratios (one player works, 4 players rest).
2. Players should always be alert and on their toes.
3. Make it competitive.
4. Variation 1 – As main drill above, but run around mannequins.
5. Variation 2 – Touch mannequin 'A', then sprint and touch mannequin 'B' and sprint past cone to finish.
6. Variation 3 – As variation 2, but go around mannequins.

10.

Speed Drill
Dash of Colour

Age group:	All age groups
Purpose:	Speed reaction drill, reacting to colours
Equipment:	8–10 mannequins and a minimum of 5 coloured cones
Duration:	Flexible
Space:	Depends on number of players
Number of participants:	Unlimited, subject to equipment and available space

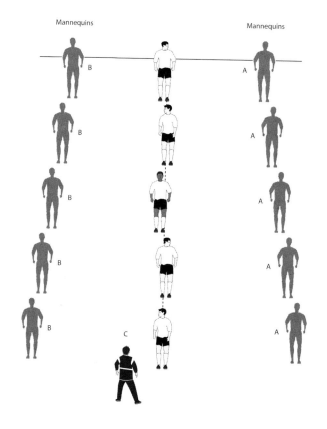

Mannequins   Mannequins

1. Distance between mannequins is your choice, depending on age group.
2. Next to each mannequin, there are placed 4–6 coloured cones. For example, line 'A' has yellow, red and blue, and line 'B' has white and green.
3. Players line up facing the coach (C).
4. Coach produces a coloured disc from behind his back – players then react to colour by sprinting to relevant mannequin, touching mannequin with their foot and sprinting back to start position.

KEY COACHING POINTS

1 Players must always be alert and on their toes.
2 Make it competitive.
3 There are many variations on this, so use your imagination.

11.

Speed Drill
Rugby Ball Relay

Age group:	12 years +
Purpose:	To improve players' speed in a competitive environment using a rugby ball
Equipment:	3 mannequins, 1 cone and 1 rugby ball per line
Duration:	Flexible
Space:	Depends on number of players
Number of participants:	Minimum 6 (2 relay lines), maximum unlimited (subject to equipment)

1. Distance between mannequins and cones is your choice, depending on age group.
2. On the drop of a ball by the coach, the first player holding the rugby ball sprints to the two mannequins at A, completes a figure of 8 and does a diving rugby throw to his team-mate, who then must go behind mannequin B with the rugby ball and repeat drill.
3. Sprint relay is completed after last man throws rugby ball to first player.

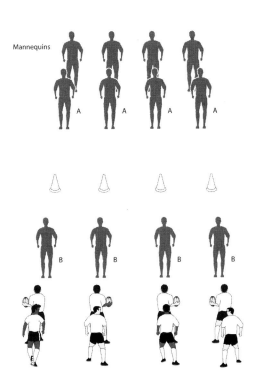

Mannequins

KEY COACHING POINTS

1. When player does figure of 8, emphasis is on dropping the shoulder on the inside turns.
2. Make it competitive.
3. Follow 'golden step' rule.
4. There are dozens of variation to this, so let your imagination run riot!

12.

Speed Drill
Ladder Crossroads
Sprints 1

Age group:	All age groups
Purpose:	To develop several components of speed, quick feet, anticipation and reaction
Equipment:	4 ladders
Duration:	Flexible
Space:	Depends on number of players and length of ladders – space between ladders at 'A' should be at least 3 x 3 m
Number of participants:	Minimum 12, maximum 24

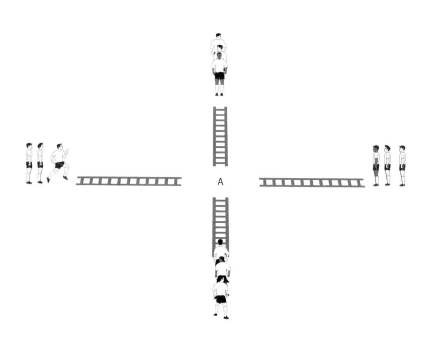

1. Ladders are positioned as shown in diagram. Players are positioned in equal numbers behind ladders.
2. One player in each group goes at the same time running through the ladder.
3. Halfway up the length of the ladder, the player steps out of the ladder and sprints to further end of the opposite ladder and rests.
4. As soon as first player steps out of ladder, second player of each group starts.
5. Players must sprint when out of the ladder and be aware of other players sprinting, hence anticipation, reaction and agility.

KEY COACHING POINTS

1. All drills are subject to foot patterns in and out of the ladder that the coach wishes to use.
2. Emphasis is on keeping the head up and not looking at your feet.
3. Feet should be working as quickly as they can in the ladders.
4. Maintaining a good posture in the ladders is important.
5. Good awareness in area 'A' is essential so that players don't hit other players in the drill.
6. There are many variations to this, not only for pattern drills but with ladder being replaced with poles, cones or mannequins, for example.

13.

Speed Drill
Ladder Crossroads
Sprints 2

Age group:	9 years +
Purpose:	To develop several components of speed, quick feet, anticipation and reaction
Equipment:	4 ladders, 1 ball
Duration:	Flexible
Space:	Depends on number of players and length of ladders – space between ladders at 'A' should be at least 8 x 8 m
Number of participants:	Minimum 12, maximum 24

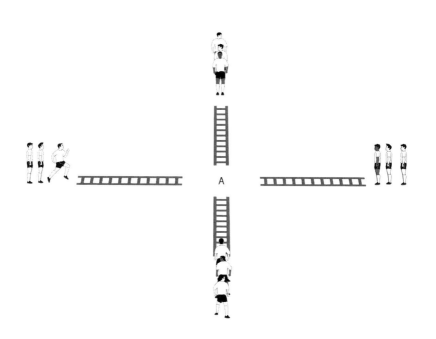

1. One player in each group goes at the same time and runs through the whole ladder. One of the four players has a ball at the end of his ladder.
2. When this player reaches the end of the ladder, he passes it to any other player reaching the centre through their own ladder.
3. First player then sprints to the end of another ladder and waits his turn. Player who passes the ball must always sprint to the group with the least number of players – this is to promote visual awareness.
4. Player receiving the ball waits until he can make his own pass to a player from another ladder.
5. As soon as each player passes the ball, the next person on his ladder starts his run through. If this is done at pace, the player receiving the ball last will always have an option to pass the ball straight away.

KEY COACHING POINTS
1. Emphasis is on keeping the head up and not looking at your feet.
2. Feet should be working as quickly as they can in the ladders.
3. Players should maintain a good posture in the ladders.
4. Quality with the ball is important.
5. Watch out for cheats!

14.

Speed Drill Figure-of-8 Baton Sprints

Age group:	All age groups
Purpose:	To do speed work in a competitive, fun way
Equipment:	3 mannequins, 1 cone and 1 baton per relay line
Duration:	Flexible
Space:	Depends on number of players
Number of participants:	Minimum of 6, maximum unlimited, subject to equipment and available space

1. First player sprints to mannequin 'C' and performs a figure of 8.
2. He then sprints back to his team-mate, who is waiting at cone 'B' (facing in the opposite direction with his back to him) ready for handover.
3. Once handover is completed, second player goes around mannequin 'A'.
4. Repeat drill until all players finished.

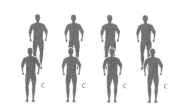

KEY COACHING POINTS

1. When player does figure of 8, emphasis is on dropping the shoulder on the inside turns.
2. Make it competitive.
3. Get the players to talk to each other, especially handing over the baton.
4. Watch out for dropped batons!
5. There are many variations on this, so you can adapt.

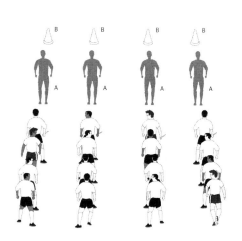

15.

Speed Drill
Shoulder to Shoulder

Age group:	9 years +
Purpose:	Competitive speed work
Equipment:	10 cones, 1 ball
Duration:	Flexible
Space:	Area used depends on age group and number of participants
Number of participants:	Minimum 3, maximum unlimited

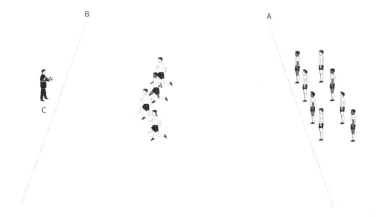

1. c =coach with ball.
2. In small groups, players start walking or jogging towards coach. Players must be shoulder to shoulder.
3. If the coach drops the ball, players sprint to finish line 'B'.
4. If the coach throws the ball up in the air, players turn and sprint back to 'A'.

KEY COACHING POINTS
1. Players should always be alert.
2. Make it competitive.
3. Beware of cheats!
4. As with other drills in this section, feel free to use variations on the same theme.

3 COACHING SKILLS AND DRILLS

Control, passing and movement – the building blocks of football

This section perhaps needs less of an introduction than the material covered in Chapter 2. Our principles and philosophies for teaching and coaching football might differ from yours. However, we hope that we stir your imagination with some of the drills in this section and make you say to yourself, 'I like that – I'll try it.'

Whether working with an individual or a group, our major aim with young players is to make them comfortable with a ball at their feet and to enjoy football training.

Footballers have two basic tools of the trade, their feet and a ball. We are great believers in working on the basics at all ages and levels, so it becomes natural without thinking about it, as the brain relocates the skills into a part where their use becomes automatic while the conscious mind thinks about other aspects. See box below for a typical example of this learning.

WHY FOOTBALL IS LIKE DRIVING

If you drive a car, you will remember what it was like the first time you went out on the road as a learner. Wasn't every junction a terror, thinking about mirrors, road position, gear changes and other motorists? You certainly would not have wanted a deep and meaningful conversation with a friend or partner in the passenger seat or to change the radio station while waiting at the traffic lights or a roundabout during your first lesson – you'd have been consciously thinking about what you had to do next to stay on the road.

Italy's Gennaro Gattuso and Fabio Cannavaro take part in a coaching drill

If you're an experienced driver today, you will be able to talk and think about other things perfectly safely while at the wheel, now that your brain has compartmentalised the basic skills of driving and you do not have to think aloud, 'Mirror, signal, manoeuvre'.

Football is much the same. A young player has to think about every kick, movement and practice drill in the beginning, but soon it becomes more intuitive and they are able to build on the basics with a greater variety of skills. Control, passing and movement are the three foundations of football. After those foundations, other skills can be added.

Learning technique early

We dislike it when we hear people we meet in football say, 'Foreign players have better technique than homegrown players' as if this is something that we cannot change. Why would that be? If they have worked hard on their technique, why have we not learned from that when there are so many overseas players in the British game? It is down to us as coaches to make time and set the standards for these basic principles with children in the limited time we have to influence them.

We must encourage young players to get out in the park practising their basic skills away from our training grounds. If you want to reach the top, there is no replacement for hard but enjoyable work, which will help turn skills into an enjoyable and natural talent. Even if you don't end up as a Cristiano Ronaldo or Francesc Fabregas – or a Hope Powell – you can still benefit hugely from combining the kind of conditioning in Chapter 2 with the drills in this chapter for a happier, healthier lifestyle.

Lastly, we would add that the techniques within the modern game – control, passing and movement – tend to be a lot more one- and two-touch tempo. Space is being closed down faster, so reaction time and speed of thought must be quicker than ever! What will happen when the young players you coach grow up in five or maybe 10 years? Will the game be slower? We doubt it.

The importance of laying the correct foundation at the right tempo, and making it enjoyable for children, is becoming more important than ever. It is our duty to make them comfortable with the ball as early as possible.

If your players are unsure how to do a drill, walk them through it with the ball in their hands first. Then try it with the ball on the ground. Start off slowly and, as players become more familiar and confident with exercise, then introduce quickness. You can therefore do so without neglecting quality.

Decision-making

As a coach, appreciate the problems the players have and try to put yourself in their position. The chances are that you were once a young footballer learning the basics – maybe you are a player still, so are having to adapt to new ways of playing and still learning skills today.

Try to understand the decisions a player has to make as he receives the ball:
- The pace of the pass will determine if he has a chance to play one-touch football or control it before delivering his own pass.
- The player must takes mental pictures of the pitch at all times to know not just where his team-mates are but also where the opposition are.
- Should he run with the ball?
- Should he cross the ball?
- Should he shoot?
- Does he volley or sidefoot the ball?

Obviously if the player is getting closed down by an opponent as he receives the ball, his decision-making time will be quicker. If under no pressure, he can 'relax' more and pick his choice with more ease.

One of your key roles in coaching the basics is to try to teach players the value of being able to make the right decisions at the right time.

Football language

Part of young players' football education is learning what we call 'smart words' that help players on the pitch. Part of their 'homework' away from training could be to write down words that they think they need on the pitch to help each other. Encourage the players to use their imagination, and give them some words to start with, like:

- 'Turn!'
- 'Man on!'
- 'Pass!'
- 'Move!'

How many more can they bring to the next training session?

Skill and technique

When asking players what they consider to be the difference between skill and technique, the answers vary quite a lot!

The definitions we use are as follows:

- **Skill** – the knowledge you have of what to do and how to do it
- **Technique** – the way you perform certain skills, e.g. headers, volleys and passing.

Don't be afraid to discuss this subject with your players and let them know what you expect of them. Young players look to please you and prove themselves to others, and you should look to encourage them at every opportunity where you think they are ready.

KEY FACTORS – WHAT YOU NEED TO BE A GOOD COACH

- **Enthusiasm** – a love of the game and job in hand.
- **Good standards** – Always praise players, but encourage them to get better – after all, what is perfection?
- **Knowledge of the game** – and not forgetting the knowledge of coaching and how players learn.

- **Patience** – sadly lacking in many coaches we have seen in action. Everybody looks for instant success as a coach. Remember that becoming the complete footballer doesn't happen overnight.
- **Time on the pitch** – The more time you can spend with your players, the better they will become!
- **Encouragement** – One of the greatest traits a coach can have is the ability to get players to enjoy football because they want to, not because you told them to. A positive attitude to every player, regardless of ability, is key.

Our belief in coaching is always to improve a player's performances. In time, this should lead to a team spirit and, if you are lucky, a winning culture.

Winning at all costs is not a great example to set – yes, you play to win, and you will do if you get more things right than wrong.

But set out your stall early when it comes to educating kids about cheating, verbal abuse of other players and officials, dangerous and violent play, and other aspects of football we would like our young people not to see on a Saturday afternoon from the family enclosure at a league ground.

Above all, try to look back on your childhood memories of organised football. From our own personal memories, we recall that we always listened to the teacher or coach we liked, rather than the one we didn't. We carried this on into football!

Now we hope that you will be able to use the following drills you like the sound of. For advice and guidance, these are broken down into basic drills suitable for all, and then by a fairly broad age range. As with the conditioning drills in Chapter 2, we would encourage you to assess carefully whether the children you are coaching in the age range in question are suited to the task in hand.

As part of the process of encouraging kids to have a great time, we asked some of the esteemed professional players we work with to lend a word or two of encouragement for you to pass on to young players about having fun and using that fun as a means to play good football. As this might best be done when you are teaching the basics, each of the first 10 drills covering basic skills that follow has words of wisdom from one of the guys that do it for a living.

Examples of a programme structure to include the drills for certain age groups is in Appendix 1 on page 186.

1. Basic Skills

Age group:	All age groups
Purpose:	To get a feel for ball, mobility
Equipment:	1 ball per pair
Duration:	5–10 mins
Space:	Variable, depending on numbers
Number of participants:	Even number, in pairs

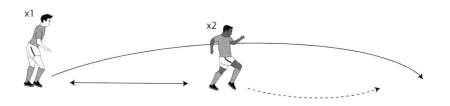

1. Players pass to each other.
2. After a given number of passes, e.g. 6, 'x2' turns away and receives a pass from 'x1' who plays into space.
3. Repeat with x1 turning.

PROGRESSION
'x2' turns with ball and plays ball into space for x1 to run on to.

'Give everything in training as you would in a game – if you improve just 1 per cent with each training session, by the end of the season you will be twice the player you were at the start!' Robert Green, West Ham and England goalkeeper

2. Basic Skills

Age group:	All age groups
Purpose:	To get a feel for the ball, mobility
Equipment:	Ball, cones for markers
Duration:	10–15 mins
Space:	10 x 10 square m
Number of participants:	4 +

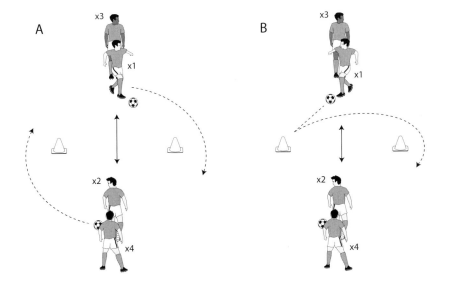

'x1' passes to 'x2' then runs around side cone to join other line of players.

PROGRESSION

'x1' passes to 'x2' then starts to run one way, but checks to go the other way. (Encourage players to imagine losing their marker.)

'Never feel you've not been trying hard enough – there's always enough time in the day to make yourself better!' Darren Huckerby, Norwich City striker

3. Basic Skills

Age group:	All age groups
Purpose:	Passing and movement
Equipment:	Balls/cones for markers
Duration:	10–15 mins
Space:	10 x 10 m square
Number of participants:	5 +

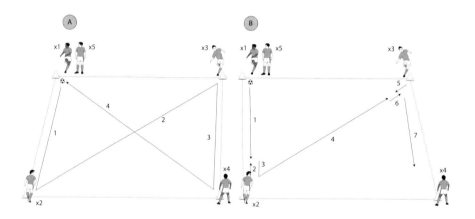

1. x1–x2/x2–x3/x3–x4
2. All players pass and follow the ball.

PROGRESSION

Play A (1–2) on every station.

> 'Be enthusiastic in training and in games, and enjoy playing football!' Mark Noble, West Ham and England U21 midfielder

4. Basic Skills

Age group:	All age groups
Purpose:	Passing and movement
Equipment:	Balls and cones
Duration:	10–15 mins
Space:	Centre circle if there is one, or circle marked with cones
Number of participants:	6 +

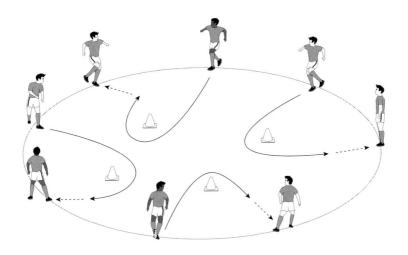

1. Players run as fast as possible and pass to a team-mate to repeat.
2. They can run around any cone and give to any team-mate.

PROGRESSION
Dribble around two cones and play 1–2.

'Approach every day with enthusiasm, and remember how lucky you are to be playing this sport with the facilities and opportunities in this country!' Alan Lee, Ipswich Town and Republic of Ireland striker

5. Basic Skills

Age group:	All age groups
Purpose:	Passing and movement
Equipment:	Balls and cones
Duration:	10–15 mins
Space:	Centre circle if there is one, or circle marked with cones
Number of participants:	4 +

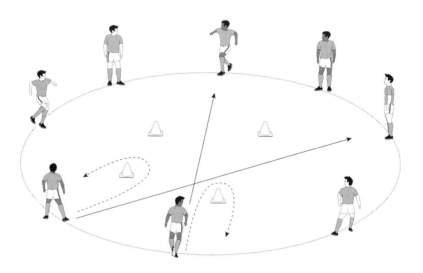

1. Pass ball in between cones to team-mate.
2. After passing, run around cone.

PROGRESSION

Man receiving ball passes to side man, who passes across.

'I enjoyed my loan period at Ipswich Town, especially the circle drills!' Mark Noble, West Ham and England U21 midfielder

6.

Basic Skills

Age group:	All age groups
Purpose:	Passing and receiving
Equipment:	Balls
Duration:	10–15 mins
Space:	20 x 30 square m
Number of participants:	3 +

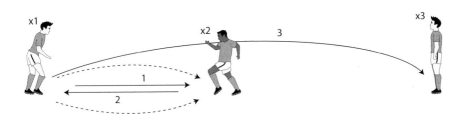

1. 'x1' plays a 1–2 with 'x2', then passes long.
2. 'x3' then repeats with 'x1'. 'x2' takes 'x1's position.

PROGRESSION

Pass in the air.

'Enjoy training! Always be enthusiastic, even when things seem to be going wrong for you.' Gavin Williams, Ipswich Town and Wales midfielder

7.   Basic Skills

Age group:	All age groups
Purpose:	Passing and receiving
Equipment:	Balls
Duration:	10–15 mins
Space:	20 x 30 square m
Number of participants:	4 +

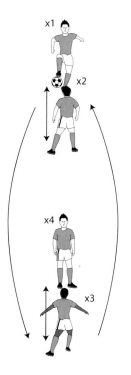

1. 'x1' plays 1–2 with 'x2', then passes long to 'x3'.
2. 'x3' plays 1–2 with 'x4' and passes long to 'x1'.

PROGRESSION

'x1' and 'x2' rotate after playing long; 'x3' and 'x4' rotate after playing long.

'When training, you must try to enjoy doing the hard bits – in a game situation against good teams, they have the ball for long periods, causing you to work hard!' Danny Haynes, Ipswich Town and England U19 striker

8. Basic Skills

Age group:	All age groups
Purpose:	Passing and movement
Equipment:	Balls and cones
Duration:	10–15 mins
Space:	10 x 10 square m
Number of participants:	4 +

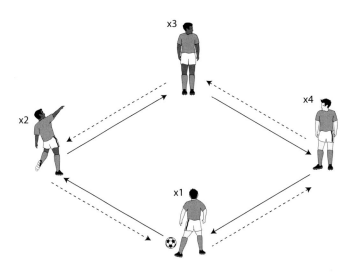

1. 'x1' passes left to 'x2', then runs to the right.
2. 'x2' passes to 'x3' (left) and runs to the right.

PROGRESSION
Pass to the right/run left

'Always believe in yourself!' Owen Garvan, Ipswich Town and Republic of Ireland U21 midfielder

9.   Basic Skills

Age group:	All age groups
Purpose:	Passing and dribbling
Equipment:	Balls and cones
Duration:	5 mins
Space:	10 x 10 square m
Number of participants:	2 +

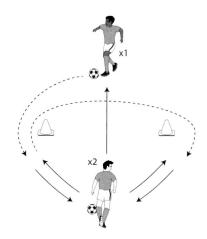

1. 'x2' passes to 'x1', who dribbles ball around cone as quickly as possible.
2. 'x1' passes to 'x2' and receives the ball back to dribble around both cones before passing to 'x2' and receiving the ball back.
3. 'x1' then dribbles the ball back around both cones and repeats the pass to 'x2'.
4. After 10 runs change over.

PROGRESSION

'x1' rounds cones and passes to 'x2', and then 'x1' runs around opposite cones (change positions).

'Be your own man, boy or girl!' Alan Lee, Ipswich Town and Republic of Ireland striker

10. Basic Skills

Age group:	All age groups
Purpose:	Passing and dribbling
Equipment:	Balls and cones
Duration:	10 mins
Space:	20 x 20 square m
Number of participants:	6 +

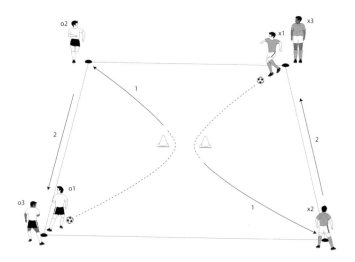

1. 'x1' and 'o1' run around cone and pass to 'x2' and 'o2'.
2. 'x1' and 'o1' follow direction of their pass.
3. 'x2' and 'o2' pass to 'x3' and 'o3' and follow their pass.
4. 'x3' and 'o3' repeat, as above.

PROGRESSION
Play a 1–2 when playing the ball into corner players.

'Through confidence and hard work you will go a long way!' Owen Garvan, Ipswich Town and Republic of Ireland U21 midfielder

1.

Technique and Skill Drill

Age group:	7–9 years
Purpose:	Attacking/Defending (1)
Equipment:	Ball, cones for line
Duration:	5–10 mins
Space:	20 x 20 m square
Number of participants:	Minimum 4

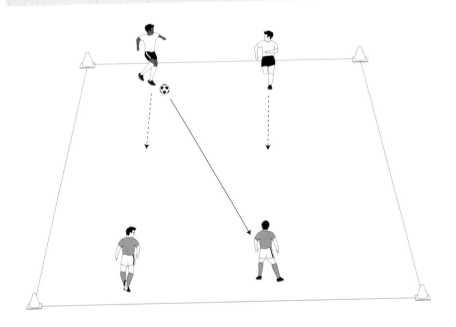

1. 2 defenders v 2 attackers.
2. Defenders close down attackers.
3. Attackers combine to get ball past defenders' line, under control.

PROGRESSION
If defenders win the ball, they then attack the opposite line to try to score!

2.

Technique and Skill Drill

Age group:	7–9 years
Purpose:	Keeping possession
Equipment:	Ball/cones for markers/bibs for defenders to hold or wear
Duration:	10–15 mins
Space:	10 x 10 m square
Number of participants:	5 +

Four players pass the ball around with one defender in the middle trying to intercept. When one player's pass is intercepted, he swaps with defender. This encourages players to keep possession of the ball.

PROGRESSION

Limit players to two touches, or one touch. Reduce number of attackers or add defenders. Ball must stay on ground.

3.

Technique and Skill Drill

Age group:	7–9 years
Purpose:	To encourage young players who are reluctant to head the ball
Equipment:	Balls, cones for markers
Duration:	10–15 mins
Space:	10 x 10 square m
Number of participants:	4 +

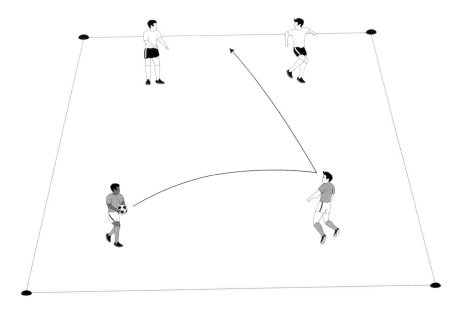

Players in pairs play 'piggy in the middle'. First player throws the ball to his partner, who heads it back over the opponents' line. Swap around when ball is intercepted.

PROGRESSION

Throw ball up and head it yourself; 1–2 headers with a team-mate; can you head straight back?

4.

Technique and Skill Drill

Age group:	7–9 years
Purpose:	To improve heading
Equipment:	Balls, goals (or cones for goalposts), bibs
Duration:	10–20 minutes
Space:	30 x 20 m square
Number of participants:	6 + (If odd numbers, extra player can 'float' for both sides – be sure to swap this player regularly)

1. Player throws ball to a team-mate to head it, then another team-mate catches it.
2. If the ball touches the floor, opposition get ball.
3. Player close enough to goal can score with a header (or head back to a team-mate to catch).

PROGRESSION

Defenders can intercept by catching the ball. The ball must not touch the floor.

5.

Technique and Skill Drill

Age group:	7–9 years
Purpose:	Attacking/Defending (2)
Equipment:	Ball, cones for lines
Duration:	5–10 minutes
Space:	10 x 20 m square
Number of participants:	Minimum 2

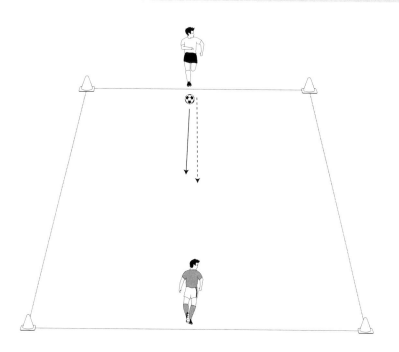

1. Defender plays ball to attacker and closes him down.
2. Attacker tries to beat defender and get ball under control past defender's line.
3. Perform drill 3 times, then swap roles.

PROGRESSION

If defender wins ball he becomes attacker and tries to dribble ball over the line.

6.

Technique and Skill Drill

Age group:	10–12 years
Purpose:	Defending and attacking
Equipment:	Balls, goals
Duration:	15–20 mins
Space:	30 x 20 m square
Number of participants:	4 + 2 goalkeepers

1. Goalkeeper throws the ball to either.
2. Player who receives ball is attacker and other one defends.
3. Receiving player attacks the goalkeeper who threw the ball.

PROGRESSION

If defender gets ball he can attack either goalkeeper.

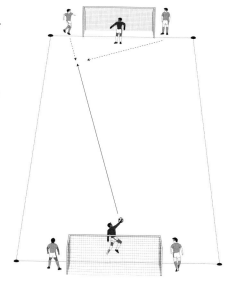

7.

Technique and Skill Drill

Age group:	10–12 years
Purpose:	Awareness of team mates and opposition
Equipment:	Balls, bibs, cones and goals
Duration:	15–20 mins
Space:	30 x 20 m square
Number of participants:	6/8 or more + 2 goalkeepers

1. This is a mini-game to encourage young players' awareness of team mates and the opposition. Give players a number.
2. Coach (C) introduces the ball at the halfway line.
3. If a player's number is called, he goes into the middle to play.
4. When other numbers are called, first player to go on runs off pitch.

PROGRESSION

All players are on the pitch.

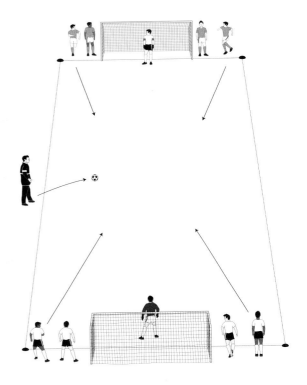

8.

Technique and Skill Drill

Age group:	10–12 years
Purpose:	Awareness/Touch/Passing
Equipment:	Balls, bibs, cones
Duration:	5–10 mins
Space:	20 x 20 m square
Number of participants:	6/8 +

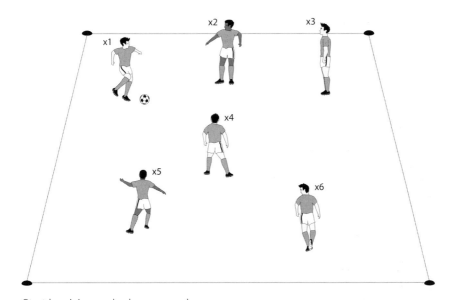

1. Start by giving each player a number.
2. Give them a ball to pass to each other in sequence of x1, x2, x3, etc.
3. 'x6' passes back to '1'.

PROGRESSION

After this becomes a simple exercise, introduce another ball to be 'thrown' in reverse order, so x6, x5, x4, etc.

9.

Technique and Skill Drill

Age group:	10–12 years
Purpose:	Passing and movement
Equipment:	Balls, bibs, cones
Duration:	10 mins
Space:	20 x 20 m square
Number of participants:	Minimum 4

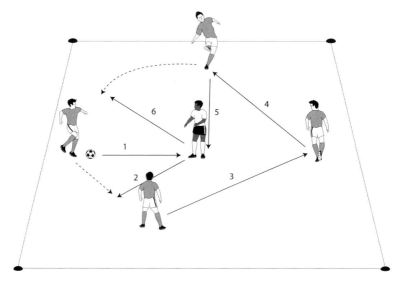

1. Pass and move anywhere inside the area.
2. When playing with the player at the centre, it must be a 1–2.

PROGRESSION

Instead of 1–2, player can feint to play 1–2, then let ball run across his body and play to someone else.

10.

Technique and Skill Drill

Age group:	10–12 years
Purpose:	Passing/Awareness
Equipment:	Balls, cones
Duration:	10–15 mins
Space:	10 x 10 m square
Number of participants:	8 +

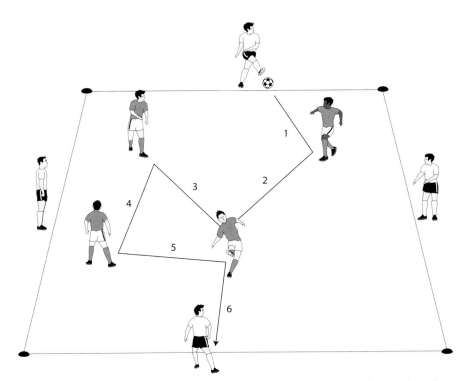

1. Players on the outside of the square play to those inside it, who combine with each other before ball goes to outside player.
2. After a set time, rotate teams.

PROGRESSION

Outside players must play to a team-mate, which starts drill again.

11.

Technique and Skill Drill

Age group: 10–12 years
Purpose: Passing over various distances
Equipment: Balls, cones
Duration: 10–15 mins
Space: 30 x 20 m square
Number of
participants: 6 +

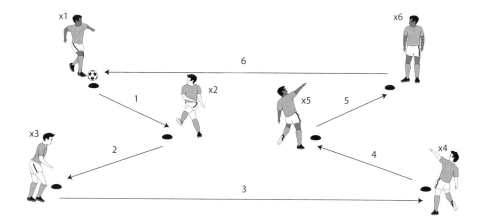

1. 'X1' passes short to 'X2'.
2. 'X2' passes short to 'X3'.
3. 'X3' passes long to 'X4'.
4. 'X4' passes short to 'X5'.
5. 'X5' passes short to 'X6'.
6. 'X6' passes long to 'X1'.
7. Repeat drill.

PROGRESSION

Encourage movement off the ball before receiving ball.

12.

Technique and Skill Drill

Age group:	10–12 years
Purpose:	Passing/Movement/Awareness
Equipment:	Balls, bibs, cones
Duration:	10–15 mins
Space:	20 x 20 square m
Number of participants:	8 +

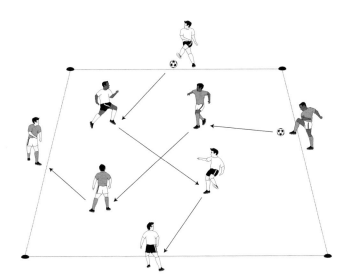

1. There are two teams, both with a ball.
2. Only pass to your team-mates, and be aware of position of other team and team-mates.
3. Each team should play from side to side as much as possible.

PROGRESSION

When you've played the ball out, follow it. Your team-mate takes the ball into the area and continues the exercise.

13.

Technique and Skill Drill

Age group: 10–12 years
Purpose: Attacking/Defending 1 v 1
Equipment: Balls, goals (or cones if unavailable), cones for marking
Duration: 10–15 mins
Space: Penalty area + 10 x 10 m square
Number of participants: 4 +

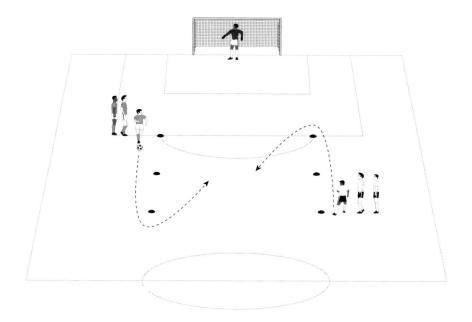

1. As soon as the player with the ball starts to run, his opponent can run around cones to defend at edge of box, 1 v 1.
2. The player with the ball must beat his opponent to score.
3. Rotate pairs often.

PROGRESSION
2 attackers v 2 defenders.

14.

Technique and Skill Drill

Age group:	10–12 years
Purpose:	Keep ball/keep away/make players comfortable with ball
Equipment:	Ball, cones for markers, bibs for defenders
Duration:	10–15 mins
Space:	Various, and depends on number of players available
Number of participants:	7 +

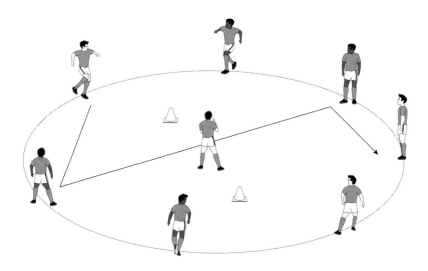

Players pass ball around avoiding interception by defenders, but cannot pass back to same player they received from. Player whose pass is intercepted swaps with that defender. This encourages players to retain possession for their team.

PROGRESSION

Limit the touches on the ball; players must move after passing; more defenders.

15.

Technique and Skill Drill

Age group:	10–12 years
Purpose:	To improve heading
Equipment:	Balls
Duration:	5–10 mins
Space:	10 X 10 m square
Number of participants:	5 +

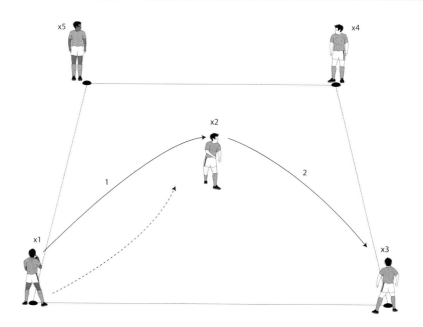

1. 'X1' throws ball to 'X2' to head to either outside player.
2. Thrower jogs into middle to receive next throw.

PROGRESSION
Receiver heads ball back in a 1–2.

16.

Technique and Skill Drill

Age group:	13–16 years
Purpose:	Passing/Movement/Awareness
Equipment:	Balls, cones
Duration:	10 mins
Space:	Centre circle or cones marked out
Number of participants:	7 +

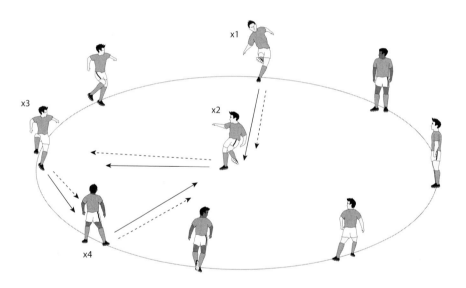

1. 'X1' passes to 'X2'.
2. 'X2' passes to 'X3' and so on, around the circle.
3. Players pass and then follow their pass to take up next position in circle.

PROGRESSION

Make each passing movement 2-touch only, then 1-touch.

17.

Technique and Skill Drill

Age group:	13–16 years
Purpose:	Ball control/Passing/ Awareness/Movement
Equipment:	2 balls, cones
Duration:	10 mins
Space:	Centre circle or cones marked out
Number of participants:	7 +

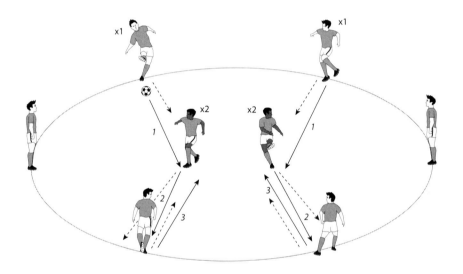

1. 'X1's pass to 'X2's. who turn and play ball out to the next player on the edge of the circle.
2. All players follow their pass to take up new position.

PROGRESSION

Outside players can play to side player. As above, they must follow the pass. As players get comfortable with the drill, introduce 2 touch and even one-touch play.

18.

Technique and Skill Drill

Age group:	13–16 years
Purpose:	To retain possession of ball
Equipment:	Balls/Bibs/Discs/ Cones
Duration:	10–15 minutes
Space:	10 x 10 m
Number of participants:	At least 8

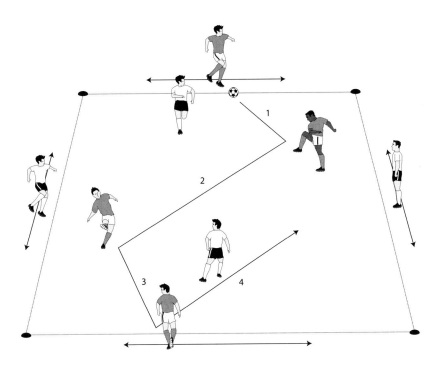

1. Players on one team combine to keep ball away from the opposite team.
2. Swap over.
3. Outside players move from side to side but are not allowed in area.

PROGRESSION

Outside players take only 1 touch.

19.

Technique and Skill Drill

Age group:	13–16 years
Purpose:	To improve crossing
Equipment:	Balls, 2 goals
Duration:	10–15 mins
Space:	40 x 40 m square
Number of participants:	4 + 2 goalkeepers

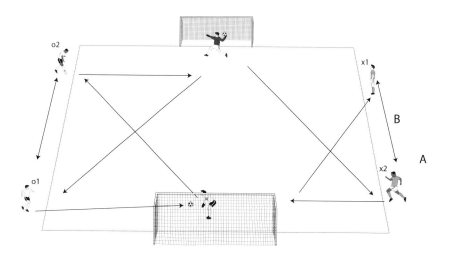

1. Goalkeepers throw ball long for receiver to control and cross ball.
2. Goalkeeper intercepts cross.
3. Once goalkeeper catches ball, repeat in opposite direction.
4. Goalies can throw either side.

PROGRESSION

After receiving the throw, instead of crossing it themselves, a player can lay ball off to a team-mate, who crosses.

20. Technique and Skill Drill

Age group:	13–16 years
Purpose:	To improve shooting
Equipment:	Balls, goals
Duration:	10–15 mins
Space:	40 x 40 m square
Number of participants:	4–6 or more + 2 goalkeepers

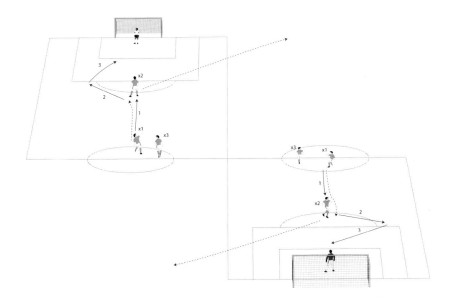

1. 'X1' passes to 'X2'. who lays to either side for 'X1' to shoot.
2. 'X1' then becomes receiver and 'X2' the shooter.

PROGRESSION

'X2' follows in for rebounds if keeper saves 'X1' shots; 'X2' plays pass in the air for 'X1' to volley shot.

21.

Technique and Skill Drill

Age group:	13–16 years
Purpose:	To improve shooting
Equipment:	Balls, goals
Duration:	10–15 mins
Space:	40 x 40 m square
Number of participants:	6 or more + 2 goalkeepers

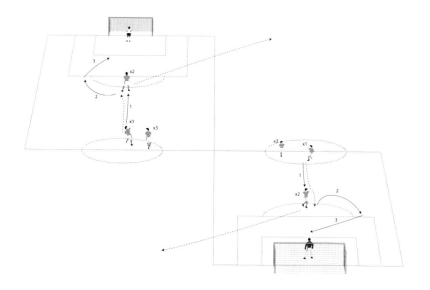

1. 'X1' passes to 'X2', who turns and shoots.
2. 'X1' takes 'X2' position.
3. 'X2' joins other group.

PROGRESSION

'X1' plays pass in the air for 'X2' to volley shot.

22.

Technique and Skill Drill

Age group:	13–16 years
Purpose:	To improve shooting
Equipment:	Balls, bibs, goals
Duration:	10–15 mins
Space:	30 x 20 m square
Number of participants:	6 + 2 goalkeepers

1. Goalkeeper throws long into opposition half for the opposition to control and shoot.
2. Players stay in their zones/areas.
3. Opposition forward can pick up any rebounds.

PROGRESSION

Players can set up a team-mate for long shot; forward player can put slight pressure on receivers; if no goalkeeper, use defender to deliver to opposite half and shoot in empty nets.

'Always enjoy it, never give up, especially when things are not going well. It's never too late to improve.'

Tommy Miller, over 250 games in the Premiership and Championship

23.

Technique and Skill Drill

Age group:	13–16 years
Purpose:	To improve shooting
Equipment:	Balls, bibs, cones, goals
Duration:	10–15 mins
Space:	30 x 20 m square
Number of participants:	6 + 2 goalkeepers

1. Players stay in their defensive zone/areas.
2. Opposition goalkeeper throws long to opposing half for the opposition to control and shoot.
3. Drill is repeated in opposite direction. Encourage long shots.

PROGRESSION

Receiver of ball from goalkeeper lays it off for one team-mate to shoot, or to receive back to shoot!

24.

Technique and Skill Drill

Age group:	13–16 years
Purpose:	Receiving skills/awareness
Equipment:	Balls
Duration:	1–2 mins
Space:	10 x 10 m square
Number of participants:	4

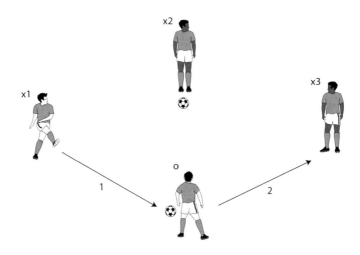

1. 3 servers have two balls between them.
2. 'X1' passes to 'o', giving to 'X3', who has no ball.
3. 'o' then looks to get ball off 'X2', etc.

PROGRESSION
Can receiver play 1-touch football?

25. Technique and Skill Drill

Age group: 13–16 years
Purpose: To improve passing/crossing
Equipment: Balls, goals, cones
Duration: 15–20 mins
Space: Penalty area
Number of participants: 6 or more + goalkeeper

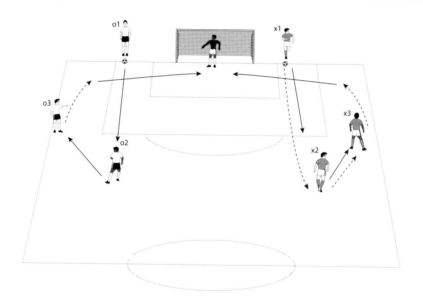

1. 'X1' passes to 'X2', who controls and gives to 'X3'.
2. 'X3' controls/dribbles and crosses into goalkeeper.
3. 'X1'/ 'X2'/ 'X3' all rotate, goalkeeper gives to 'O1' to repeat on other side.

PROGRESSION

Movement off ball to receive pass.

26.

Technique and Skill Drill

Age group:	13–16 years
Purpose:	Passing/Receiving/Awareness/Keep ball
Equipment:	Balls, bibs, cones
Duration:	10–15 mins
Space:	20 x 20 m square
Number of participants:	6 +

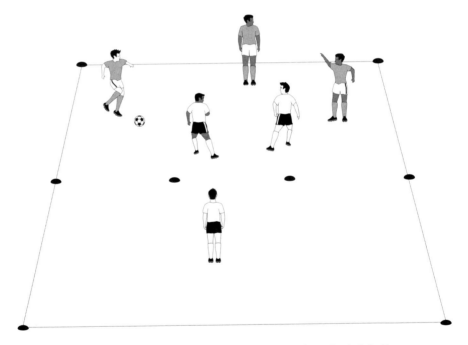

1. Two teams play in one half. Defending team leave one player in their half.
2. If defenders recover the ball, they transfer ball back into their half. The other team then leave one player back and the play moves to the other half.

PROGRESSION

Limit number of passes to attacking team.

27.

Technique and Skill Drill

Age group:	13–16 years
Purpose:	Passing and shooting
Equipment:	Balls, cones if no goals
Duration:	10–15 mins
Space:	Penalty area
Number of participants:	6 + goalkeeper

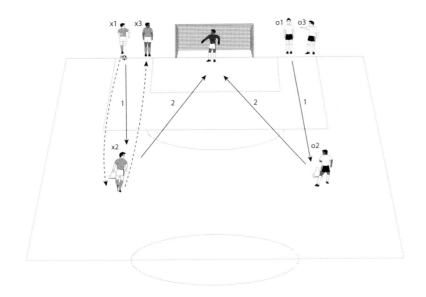

1. 'X1' plays ball to edge of box for 'X2' to run on to and shoot at goal. (If no goalkeeper, hit an empty goal.)
2. 'X1' follows to 'X2' position, 'X2' after shot changes position. 'O's repeat on opposite side.

PROGRESSION
'X1' and 'X2' play quick 1–2 on edge of area before shooting.

28.

Technique and Skill Drill

Age group:	13–16 years
Purpose:	Keep ball/keep away/ make players comfortable with the ball
Equipment:	Balls, bibs, cones for markers
Duration:	10–20 mins
Space:	30 x 20 square m
Number of participants:	Minimum 8

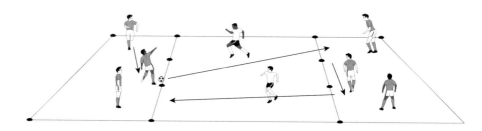

1. All players are restricted to their zones.
2. Team with ball combine to keep it and get ball across to team-mates without defenders touching ball.
3. Whoever gives ball away switches with defender.

PROGRESSION

Limit players to fewer touches, eg. 2-touch. After a nominated number of passes, ball must be played across; ball must stay on the ground.

29.

Technique and Skill Drill

Age group:	13–16 years
Purpose:	Attacking/Defending game
Equipment:	Ball, bibs, cones, goals
Duration:	10–20 mins
Space:	30 x 40 m square
Number of participants:	At least 6 (if no goalkeepers, players alternate being in goal)

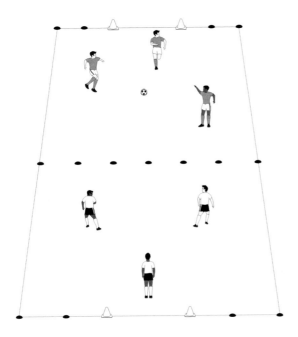

Players simply play against each other to improve attacking/defending, and encourage taking defenders on.

PROGRESSION

You can only score in opponents' defending half, your attacking half!

30.

Technique and Skill Drill

Age group: 13–16 years
Purpose: Passing drill for movement and touch
Equipment: Balls
Duration: 10–15 mins
Space: Centre circle
Number of participants: 4 +

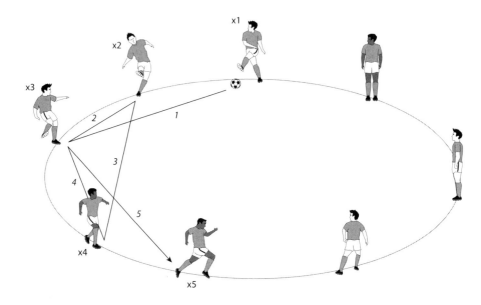

'X1' plays to 'X3', 'X2' to 'X4', etc. Passes miss the adjacent player out.

PROGRESSION

Movement away from ball and back to lay off to team-mate. Add more balls to keep the drill fast-paced.

4 NUTRITION

Food and fluid are our body's fuel. To achieve good health for the future, and a high level of fitness and performance, it is crucial to get your nutritional intake right.

Children taking part in sport offer more of a challenge, as they are still growing and developing. Not only do they require the right balance of nutrition for sports performance, but they also need to meet the nutritional requirements for their age.

We'll begin this chapter by covering basic nutrition for this age group and why food choices are important for football. This will bring you up to speed and inform you on the scientific background to the advice and suggestions given later on. Further topics cover a huge range of food issues when working with young players.

We have also included case studies to give examples of how the advice has been put into practice successfully. Suggestions for pre- and post-match snacks and meals are made.

Suggested daily menus will be given for home and away games at varying kick-off times; these sample menus can be found in the appendices at the end of Chapter 5 on pages 190–200. Food choices for travelling are also covered.

Our approach to food is that it should be enjoyed. There are many influences that dictate what we eat, and this is more of a factor for the younger age group. These influences will be explored, and guidance given on managing these while still making appropriate food choices.

Children need the flexibility and freedom to enjoy their food. This chapter will not offer advice in a dictatorial way, but in a fun, practical way that offers informed choice.

We believe that education and skills-based learning empowers children, parents and those running football learning environments to self-manage their food choices. You can then feel confident that you can maximise young players' training and playing performance.

The basics

To achieve good health for the future and for a high level of fitness and performance in your football, it is important to understand more about the food you eat. This will help you make the right food choices at meal and snack times. This chapter also offers parents, carers, coaches and others involved in training young footballers more of an insight into the basics of nutrition and the type of diet that is crucial for a growing footballer.

One of the tricky things about trying to eat well is the time of training and games. Add on travelling and it can mean that usual mealtimes go out the window. So planning and organising your day and what, when and where you will eat is very important.

First things first
There are three main food groups that our food fits into. These are:
- Carbohydrate
- Protein
- Fat

Most foods contain a mixture of these, e.g. biscuits contain fat and carbohydrate (in the form of sugar and flour), meat contains fat and protein, milk contains carbohydrate and fat. So, foods can be grouped into more than one food group.

Each food group provides different things for the body, so a mixture of these foods needs to be eaten. You will not get everything your body needs from one of them. It is getting the mixture right that is crucial to health and performance on the field. (See Tips for a balanced diet on pages 154–8.)

Energy
Energy is commonly measured in kilocalories (Kcal), more commonly known simply as 'calories', and the body gets energy from burning carbohydrate, protein and fat. The main source of energy for the body is carbohydrate and it is the most important energy source for peak football performance.

In equal amounts each food group provides different amounts of energy.
- 1g of carbohydrate will provide 3.45 Kcal
- 1g of protein will provide 4 Kcal
- 1g of fat will provide 9 Kcal

However, carbohydrate is still the body's best source of fuel for exercise. If you eat a high-fat diet, it will not provide you with more energy for your football, but will instead quickly lead to excess energy that the body will not use. It will be stored as body fat, contributing to unwanted weight gain.

Carbohydrate

Carbohydrate is the body's most important source of energy during exercise, and it is made up of sugar and starch. All carbohydrates are broken down in the stomach into glucose, a type of sugar. Glucose is the source of energy used by your muscles and the brain. All carbohydrates break down into glucose at different rates and it is the ones that break down slowly which are important, as they release energy slowly and steadily. This is referred to as the Glycaemic Index (GI). See the section on 'The GI of Carbs' on pages 159–61.

As carbohydrates are sugars and starches, we can classify foods into these two groups, as shown in Table 4.1. There are times when foods appear in both groups, as they contain a mixture of sugar and starch.

Sugar provides nothing more than energy (Kcal), which is instant and not sustained. Foods like sweets, chocolate, biscuits and cake provide no other vitamins or minerals, just energy. They can be useful to top up your energy needs, but your main source of energy should come from starchy foods.

Starchy foods provide longer-lasting energy, fibre, iron and B vitamins. They should be the main part of every meal (breakfast, lunch and dinner). Eating meals high in starchy carbohydrates means that you are always

TABLE 4.1	FOOD CLASSIFICATION – STARCHES AND SUGARS
STARCHES	**SUGARS**
Breads (sliced bread, rolls, bagels, French stick, etc.)	Sugar
	Preserves (jam and marmalade)
Pasta	Honey
Rice	Sweets
Potatoes	Chocolate
Crisps	Biscuits
Noodles	Cakes
Breakfast Cereal	Milk
Pulses (beans and lentils)	Yoghurt
Flour	Fromage Frais
Pastry	Fruit
Biscuits	Fruit Juice
Cakes	Ice-cream
	Puddings

topping up your body's energy levels ready for the next game or training session.

Remember that although crisps, pastry, cake and biscuits all contain starch, they also contain fat and/or sugar and are therefore not the preferred sources of energy for any exercise. Keep these minimal and concentrate on the foods which are nearly pure starch, e.g. breads, cereal, potatoes, rice, pasta and noodles. These foods can also be useful as snacks between meals, e.g. toast and Marmite or cereal before bed.

The amount of carbohydrate young people need each day varies hugely depending on their age and exercise level. You do not need to be counting the amounts of carbohydrate that they eat, but if they are growing well and maintaining a healthy weight, let their appetite dictate.

Maintaining a healthy weight while growing

If you (or a coach) feel a young player needs to lose weight, ask a doctor to confirm this. Adult versions of working out if someone is overweight or underweight, e.g. Body Mass Index (BMI), cannot be used on children, as they do not take into account growth. Growth (weight and height) can be plotted on growth charts for gender and age, which will assess if a child needs to be more careful with their weight or if they need to increase their food intake to help gain weight. If they do need to be more careful with their weight, see if you can make any healthy changes to their diet and/or increase their exercise level. Sometimes it is beneficial to keep their weight steady while they grow taller, rather than trying to lose weight. Be sensible and always get professional advice.

Body image is important to many, especially in sport, to gain approval from coaches and peers, and for success in the sport. As a result, actions can be taken too far and result in negative effects on weight, body image and performance. Always seek professional advice and reassurance for any young person affected by these factors. See Case Study B on page 203 as an example of how comments from influential people can have a detrimental effect on a person's actions without appropriate advice.

Protein

The body (especially our muscles) uses protein to grow, develop and repair itself. So, protein foods are crucial while you are growing. Protein foods also contain iron and fat, but you can reduce the amount of fat you get from these foods. (See 'Tips on cooking' on page 167 and the section on Fats on page 152.) We get protein from the foods listed in Table 4.2 below.

Taking part in regular exercise can mean that you require slightly greater amounts of protein but, generally, we all eat more than enough protein for

TABLE 4.2	FOOD CLASSIFICATION – PROTEIN
TYPE	**EXAMPLES**
Meat	*Beef*
	Pork
	Chicken
	Turkey
	Lamb
Meat Products	Sausages
	Burgers
	Meat pies
Fish	*White fish*
	Oily fish
	Shellfish
Milk	
Yoghurt	
Cheese	
Fromage Frais	
Eggs	
Pulses (Beans and Lentils)	Baked beans
	Kidney beans
	Butter beans
Nuts	
Tofu	
Quorn and Soya Products	

Note: Some of these foods are better sources of protein than others for the body. The best ones are italicised in the table.

our body's needs, so there is no need to eat more protein or take protein supplements.

Protein is needed every day and you will reach your protein requirements if you include two main sources a day. (See the section on 'Tips for a balanced diet' on page 154.) If your body gets more than it needs it will convert it into energy to be used by the body or to be stored as fat, but the body's best source of energy is carbohydrate, as previously mentioned, so excess protein is a very inefficient source of energy.

The best way to make sure that the protein you are eating is being used to develop the muscles used in exercise is to ensure that you eat enough carbohydrate. A lack of carbohydrate and energy will mean that the body has to use the protein for energy. The protein will then not be available for the muscle to grow and develop.

Muscle development and strength is not only gained by eating an adequate diet, but is gained in combination with resistance exercise. (See resistance exercises in Chapter 2.)

Fats

Although fat is thought of as the bad guy, we do actually need fat in our diet. It provides the body with a layer of warmth and some essential vitamins, and it is important for maintaining a number of the body's functions. The problem is that we are all eating too much fat, both adults and children. As is well documented and commented on just about everywhere, excessive fat intake leads to weight gain and can cause health problems later on in life, or even when people are young.

TABLE 4.3	FATS	
SATURATED FATS (Animal origin)	**UNSATURATED FATS** (Plant Origin)	
	Poly-Unsaturated Fats ✔	Mono-Unsaturated Fats ✔ ✔
✘		
Butter Lard Suet Dripping Cheese Cream Milk Meat Meat Products	Sunflower oil Some vegetable oils Spreads made from sunflower oil	Olive oil Rapeseed oil Some vegetable oils Spreads containing olive oil or vegetable oil

There are also different kinds of fats and it is important that we eat the right type of fat for our health. Fats can be divided into two main groups:
- Saturated
- Unsaturated

Table 4.3 details 'bad' (saturated, animal-based) and 'good' (unsaturated, plant-based) fats for a healthy diet and what foods are classified as containing them. We've also broken down the unsaturated fats into their two groups.

One thing to remember is that in equal amounts, e.g. one tablespoon of lard compared with one tablespoon of olive oil, all the types of fat contain the same amount of energy, but can have quite different effects on your long-term health. If you want to watch your weight, be careful with how much you use, regardless of whether it is a saturated or unsaturated fat.

Saturated Fat – Red Card!

The body finds it hard to break down saturated fat and so it stores it. It lines the arteries around the body, which reduces the space for bloodflow and increases blood pressure. It is a bit like having a kink in a hosepipe. Saturated fat also increases cholesterol levels in the blood. All this can lead to problems with the health of the heart, heart attacks and strokes in the long term. One way to spot them is to remember that saturated fats are solid at room temperature.

Unsaturated fat – Play on!

The body is able to break down these fats and so they do not cause the health problems that saturated fats do. These fats are liquid at room temperature.

Oily Fish

Oily fish, e.g. salmon, fresh tuna, mackerel, herring and pilchards, contain a type of poly-unsaturated fat known as omega-3. These are beneficial to health and should be eaten twice a week. Note that, unfortunately, tinned tuna does not provide this essential omega-3 – it is lost in the canning process.

Iron

Iron is important to ensure that your blood cells can carry oxygen around your body. The muscles use oxygen to work during exercise, so it is important that foods containing iron are included daily in young players' diet to ensure they are at their peak for playing and training. If you don't get enough iron, you can feel tired, irritable and find it difficult to concentrate. This can lead to a lack of energy and bad decisions on the field.

There are foods that have been fortified with iron and therefore provide extra iron, e.g. breakfast cereals like corn flakes, but the best sources of iron are protein foods, especially red meats because they contain a form of iron that is easily absorbed. Other sources include oily fish, dark green leafy vegetables and beans. Vitamin C helps the body to absorb iron and so it is a good idea to eat a meal that contains meat, for example, with a food or drink that contains vitamin C, e.g. fruit juice, fruit or vegetables.

It is especially important that girls are eating plenty of sources of iron, as they have higher requirements than boys during growth and development.

Calcium

Calcium is essential for the growth, development and strength of your teeth and bones. Milk and dairy products are the best sources of calcium. These will strengthen your bones now and for the future, reducing your risk of osteoporosis later on in life.

Fibre

There are two types of fibre, soluble and insoluble, and both have different roles to play in the body.

Foods containing soluble fibre include fruit, vegetables and pulses (lentils and beans). This fibre works in the blood to help control cholesterol levels and blood glucose levels.

Foods containing insoluble fibre include high-fibre starchy foods, e.g. wholemeal bread (rather than white bread), Weetabix or Shreddies (rather than Rice Krispies or cornflakes). These foods help the stomach and intestines to work properly and help prevent constipation. You also need to drink plenty to avoid or relieve this problem.

Tips for a balanced diet

Getting the balance of energy from carbohydrate, protein and fat together with nutrients and vitamins is essential for optimum growth and development throughout your childhood years.

The Eatwell Plate (shown in Figure 4.1), devised by the Food Standards Agency, shows you the right balance between food groups for all the nutrition you need every day.

FIGURE 4.1 **THE EATWELL PLATE**

Adapted from Food Standards Agency website, www.eatwell.gov.uk

Bread, rice, potatoes, pasta and other starchy foods

This group includes all the starchy carbohydrates, breads, rice, potatoes, pasta, noodles, breakfast cereal and any other grains, e.g. semolina, tapioca. As you can see, this group is one of the largest and makes up around a third of your daily food intake. Include these foods at each meal and base snacks on these foods too, e.g. cereal bars, toasted bagel, toast and jam. Try to include varieties that are high in fibre and low GI, e.g. granary bread instead of white bread. These foods are naturally low in fat and high in footballers' energy.

Fruit and vegetables

This food group includes salad and is also one of the largest, making up another third of your daily food intake. So, include them at each meal and use them for snacks. These foods are extremely high in a complete range of vitamins and minerals. They are also a good source of fibre (soluble). You will probably have heard the 'five-a-day healthy lifestyle' message already from various corners of the mass media – to ensure you include all the vitamins and minerals the child's body needs, they should eat at least five portions of a variety of different-coloured fruits and vegetables each day. This does not mean five portions of fruit and also five portions of vegetables every day, but a combination that adds up to five, e.g. two portions of fruit and three portions of vegetables, or one portion of fruit and four portions of vegetables. See box for details of what 'a portion' actually equates with:

The portions for younger children may be smaller – as a guide, a child's handful would be equal to a portion. Children's appetites can always move on to adult portions quite quickly! Older children usually consume adult portions without any problems.

What doesn't count – sorry !

- Fruit-flavoured drinks and squashes
- Fruit yoghurt

WHAT IS 'ONE PORTION' OF OUR 'FIVE-A-DAY'?

- One piece of fruit, e.g. an apple, orange, pear, banana
- Two smaller fruits, e.g. two plums, two satsumas, two kiwi fruits
- A cup or handful of berries, e.g. grapes, strawberries
- Half to one tablespoon of dried fruit, e.g. raisins, apricots
- Two to three tablespoons of fruit salad, cooked or canned fruit
- Half a grapefruit
- A wedge of melon
- Two rings of pineapple
- One glass of fruit juice*
- A bowl of mixed salad
- Two tablespoons of raw or cooked (frozen, canned or fresh) vegetables.

These portions are for adults and are based on five 80 g portions, which is equal to 400 g of fruit and vegetables each day.

*This one only counts once a day, so if you drink more, it won't count as more.

- Fruit and Nut chocolate
- Jam/marmalade
- Tomato ketchup
- Potatoes – these may be a vegetable, but are counted as a starchy food!

Meat, fish, eggs, beans and other non-dairy sources of protein

This food group shows us our main sources of protein and iron, including those for a vegetarian diet. They include all meats, fish (white and oily) and shellfish, eggs, pulses (beans and lentils), nuts, tofu, Quorn and soya products.

The proportion on the Eatwell Plate means including a lean source of protein twice a day, e.g. a ham/chicken/tuna sandwich or baked beans on toast at lunch, and lean pork, grilled beef steak, grilled salmon or omelette as part of a meal at dinnertime. This will ensure that the child gets the protein and iron requirements their body needs. Added protein will come from the dairy foods you eat, e.g. milk on your cereal, yoghurt with your lunch.

One important thing to remember is that these foods can contribute a lot of fat to the diet. So choose lean meats and remove visible fat. Do not be tempted to serve up pork crackling and crispy chicken skin. Kids will probably love them, but these are pure saturated fat.

Milk and dairy foods

This group includes milk, yoghurt, fromage frais, soya milk and cheese, varying from hard cheese to soft cheese, cheese spread and cottage cheese. These foods provide protein and are our main sources of calcium. Calcium is needed for the growth, development and strength of your bones and teeth. The proportion on the Eatwell Plate means including these foods two to three times each day, e.g. milk on cereal, a yoghurt after lunch, and cheese and biscuits as an afternoon snack.

These foods can be high in fat, so choose low-fat varieties and in some instances, i.e. cheese, watch how much you use. You can also reduce the amount of cheese you use if you grate it, rather than slicing it.

Choose low fat milk, e.g. semi-skimmed or skimmed, low-fat yoghurts and low-fat cheese spreads. See the section on labelling (page 171) to find out how you can check that foods are low in fat.

Foods and drinks high in fat and/or sugar

This group includes butter, margarine, spreads, suet, cooking fats and oils, pastry (i.e. sausage rolls, pork pies, quiche, meat pies, apple pies), cakes, sweets, chocolate, biscuits, crisps, chips, meat products, bacon, traditional puddings and desserts, ordinary squash and fizzy drinks.

As the Eatwell Plate shows, this section of foods makes up the smallest part of your daily diet. These foods should be eaten sparingly in the day and should be kept to treats or special occasions.

There are lots of ways you can lower the fat and sugar content of these foods.

1. Choose lower-fat or sugar alternatives available in the shops, e.g. 'no added sugar' squash, diet cola, low-fat spreads, low-fat crisps, low-sugar jelly.
2. Reduce the amount of spread you put on bread and toast. Consider whether a child really needs spread in their sandwiches when you have other things to make it moist and tasty, e.g. pickle or salad cream, or do they need spread on their toast when you've put baked beans on top?
3. Reduce the amount of vegetable/olive/sunflower oil used when cooking.
4. Choose methods of cooking that reduce the natural fat content of the food, e.g. grilling, poaching, steaming or baking instead of frying or roasting with cooking fat. See the section on cooking tips (pages 167–170).
5. Watch the frequency that you eat these foods. Remember that, although the child might only have crisps three times a week, a burger and fries on a Saturday in town, cake at the weekend, biscuits every mid-morning, a normal cola and an ice-cream on a Friday night, a chocolate bar twice a week and a chicken pie once a week, these foods all add up. These foods may differ in terms of how they look and taste, but to a growing body they all have two things in common, and that is fat and sugar.
6. Reduce portion sizes, e.g. regular fries instead of extra large fries, a normal bag of crisps rather than the larger 'grab bag' size, or a 'snack size' chocolate bar instead of a standard-sized one.

Use the Eatwell Plate to see how the child's diet matches up. Do you think what they eat in a day matches the proportion on the plate?

Further tips

Salt

Don't add salt to food while cooking or let kids add it at the table. If they cannot do without it, either add it while cooking or at the table, but not both. Try to use less too. We all get plenty of salt in our diet from the foods that we eat. There are many foods that naturally contain salt, e.g. bacon, ham, cheese and many foods that have been made by manufacturers that have added salt, which we can then not remove, e.g. crisps, sausages, soup.

Children need less salt than adults. The maximum suggested intake for

TABLE 4.4	RECOMMENDED MAXIMUM DAILY SALT INTAKE
AGE	**AMOUNT (G)**
4–6 years	3
7–10 years	5
11 years +	6

adults is six grams a day. The maximum amount for children varies depending on age, as shown in Table 4.4.

Nowadays, labels often tell you how much sodium is in the product. Sodium is itself a metallic element and not salt as you find it in food products – salt's proper name is sodium chloride. Therefore you need to do a little maths:

Salt = sodium x 2.5

You can then compare this to the amount recommended per day for the child.

Fluid

Make sure children drink plenty. For good health they should be drinking at least six to eight glasses (approx 200 ml) of fluid each day. This should mainly come from water. You can also have 'no added sugar' squashes and diet fizzy drinks. Tea and coffee will not hydrate the body as well as these drinks, so they should drink less of these by comparison. Milk, fruit juice and smoothies are great nutritional drinks, but again will not hydrate you as well.

Let them enjoy a varied diet!

We've already said how important it is to make training and games interesting so that kids enjoy football – eating and drinking should also be enjoyable, so use as much imagination as you can when preparing healthy meals, drinks and snacks.

Glycaemic index (GI)

The Glycaemic index is all about how quickly or slowly a food breaks down into glucose and is absorbed. Individual foods have been tested to assess this and have then been given a number from 0 to 100.

Foods with a high number have a high GI. These foods break down quickly, releasing energy instantly. However, this energy is not sustained and so you can feel tired and hungry very soon afterwards.

TABLE 4.5	FOOD CLASSIFICATION – GI
LOW–MEDIUM-GI FOODS ✔ ✔	**HIGH-GI FOODS** ✔
Wholegrain breads (granary and multigrain varieties)	White and brown breads
Oats (porridge)	Cornflakes
Muesli	Rice Krispies
Special K (original)	Glucose
All-Bran	Sugar
Bran Flakes	Sports drinks
Weetabix	Ordinary drinks, e.g. cola, lemonade, original squash
Shredded Wheat	Mashed potato
All low-fat dairy products	Jacket potato
Beans, lentils and pulses	Watermelon
Vegetables and salad	White and brown rice, apart from those in the opposite list
Basmati rice	
Wild rice	
Pasta	
Instant noodles	
Sweet potato	
New/boiled potatoes	
Bananas	
Apples	
Pears	
Plums	
Peaches	
Oranges	
Popcorn	
Couscous	

Foods with a low number have a low GI. These foods break down slowly, releasing energy over time. They sustain energy levels and keep you feeling fuller for much longer.

Foods in between are termed 'medium GI'.

A young footballer requires more low GI foods than high GI foods for meals and snacks on a day-to-day basis.

Low-GI carbohydrates eaten daily will ensure energy levels are sustained for when training and playing games. Eating plenty of these low-GI carbohydrates will also mean glycogen stores remain fully stocked up. See section on fuel for football.

High-GI carbohydrates are useful in the dressing room, immediately before and after a match.

There are many books out there on GI, and it has many uses. It is not a diet in itself, but a way of knowing more about your food and how it can benefit you. These low-GI choices should then be fitted in with the principles for a balanced diet.

GI can be used to aid weight loss, heart health, diabetes management and, importantly, sports performance.

You do not need to completely avoid high-GI foods. Combining a low- and a high-GI food will give you a meal with a medium GI. Remember these foods have been tested individually and once we eat them in combination, at a meal, we can get a whole different GI effect.

Our top tip is to always include a low-GI food at each meal. This food will then reduce the GI for the whole meal, e.g. baked beans (low GI) added to toast made from white bread (high GI) will give a medium-GI effect.

You would imagine that, when it comes to carbohydrates, sugary foods were high GI and starchy foods were low GI. Table 4.5 shows that this is not always the case and gives examples of foods that are high and those that are low–medium. The reasons why foods may have a different GI to the one you imagined are many and varied. If you want to know more there are many books available on the subject.

Fuel for football

Glycogen stores

As discussed, carbohydrates are the body's source of energy during exercise. On a day-to-day basis, the carbohydrates that you eat are being broken down into glucose. This glucose is used for your daily activities, but some of the glucose is stored in the liver and muscles as glycogen (as discussed in Chapter 2, page 31 on muscle type development). Glycogen is your body's main store of energy.

When you exercise, initial energy will come from what you have just recently had to eat or drink. As the exercise goes on your body will convert the stored glycogen back into glucose for the muscle to use as energy. This means you are able to play well!

How do we make sure we have enough glycogen?

To make sure that kids have sufficient energy stored in their bodies as glycogen, they need to eat carbohydrate with each meal every day. They can also have carbohydrate snacks, e.g. cereal bars, bananas. This will make sure they have the energy they need when they train and play. The food and drink they eat just before a game will not give their body enough energy for 90 minutes' exercise!

What happens if we don't have enough glycogen?

Not having enough glycogen stored in your liver and muscles will occur if you are not eating enough carbohydrate on a day-to-day basis. It will also happen if you are not refuelling well enough (see 'Refuelling' on page 164).

As a result, muscles will not have the energy children need while they are playing and training. This will result in their:
• feeling tired and having less energy
• being unable to play a full 90 minutes
• feeling a drop in concentration levels
• being unable to make accurate decision on the field
• being more likely to get injured.

If their diet is not providing them with what they need and they are injured, their body will take longer to recover. (See section on 'considerations when injured', page 173.)

Pre-match meal/snacks

A low-fat, high-carbohydrate meal or snack two to three hours before a match will top up their energy stores. Two to three hours will also allow time for the food to digest and the stomach to empty appropriately. This will prevent players from feeling bloated and uncomfortable, and getting a stitch while playing.

What you have as a pre-match meal will depend on the time of kick-off and the distance you need to travel. If you are playing mid-morning, e.g. 11 o'clock, then your pre-match meal should be your breakfast and then a top-up snack an hour before kick-off. See box below for a typical suggestion. If you are playing mid-afternoon, e.g. 3 o'clock, then your pre-match meal should be an early lunch, e.g. midday, with a top-up snack an hour before kick-off, as suggested below.

Snacks in the dressing room

Just before they play, young players can benefit from some fast-acting energy to give them that initial boost on the pitch. Once they are into play, their

BUILD-UP TO A MID-MORNING MATCH

- Cereal (high fibre and low-GI), e.g. Weetabix or Shreddies, with milk (skimmed or semi-skimmed)
- A yoghurt
- A toasted raisin-and-cinnamon bagel
- A glass of fruit juice.

or

- Cereal (high-fibre and low-GI), e.g. porridge, Bran Flakes, with sliced banana and milk
- Scrambled egg and baked beans on granary toast (high-fibre and low-GI)
- A glass of fruit juice.

plus a top-up snack, for example:
- Cereal bar
- Banana and a glass of milk
- Currant bun.

bodies will start converting the stored glycogen into the glucose they need to continue playing.

See the section on fluid (pages 173–5) for ideas about what to drink and when, but here are some ideas for snacks in the dressing room.
- Handful of jelly beans or jelly babies
- Fruit juice (approx. 150–200 ml carton)
- Mini chocolate bar, e.g. mini Mars or Milky Way.

BUILD-UP TO A MID-AFTERNOON MATCH

- Jacket potato with tuna, mayonnaise and sweetcorn
- A side salad
- Fresh fruit salad and yoghurt.

or

- Chicken pasta bake with salad or vegetables
- Banana and custard.

Topping up at half time

The same snacks and drink can be used at half time as in the dressing room just before. Another boost of energy is needed for the second half.

The same can be applied to training sessions at the beginning and mid-point of a session.

Refuelling/Post-match snacks

After a game, glycogen stores will be empty, so it is important to replenish these as quickly as possible. Players will then be at their best for the next training session or game. The glycogen stores are best replenished within the first few hours after training or a game.

The best foods to eat as post-match snacks are high-carbohydrate, for example:

- Sandwiches, with a variety of fillings, e.g. tuna and salad, ham and tomato, cheese and pickle, chicken and avocado, cream cheese and chutney, etc.
- Teacake
- Malt loaf
- Banana
- Cereal bar
- Toast
- Bagel
- Cereal and milk
- Fruit (fresh or dried)
- Flapjack
- Biscuits
- Yoghurt
- Milkshake, yoghurt drink or smoothie.

Don't forget to get players to drink plenty to rehydrate too. (The above drinks will not be sufficient to replenish the body with the fluid it needs.) See section on fluid on page 173.

Avoid grabbing a quick takeaway on the way home after a game, e.g. fish and chips, pizza, fried chicken. Have a meal planned! See the section on 'Tips for planning ahead' below.

Tips for a footballer's diet

Playing football means you need to eat a balanced, healthy diet, whatever age or level you are at. Knowing more about your food, as we have discovered in earlier sections of this chapter, means you can make informed choices about what players eat and when. These choices will aid their growth and development as well as their sports performance and fitness levels.

As a young football player, they also need to know about carbohydrates, refuelling, fluid and what to eat pre- and post-match and training to ensure they can be at their very best, so remember to educate them as to why they are eating different foods at different times.

The below box contains top tips for a young footballer's diet. You could copy this and put it on your fridge so that the young footballer in your household sees it every time they fancy raiding it for something!

YOUNG FOOTBALLERS' TOP TIPS

- Always have breakfast. Regular meals are important and breakfast is a crucial meal of the day. It will ensure you get the energy and nutrition you need to avoid tiredness and hunger and to improve concentration levels and smart decisions, needed both for school and on the training pitch.
- Avoiding breakfast will mean you haven't 'broken' the 'fast' (hence the word 'breakfast'), which is what your body has gone through overnight. Your body will be running on empty and you will not have topped up the glycogen stores in your body. You will not be at your best on the pitch!
- Include those all-important carbohydrates at each meal and base snacks on them too. These carbs should be high-fibre and low-GI and will keep your glycogen and energy levels stocked up ready for a top performance.
- Organise and plan ahead. This will involve your parents, coaches and you! Kick-off times, training times and travelling times can change usual mealtimes. This doesn't mean you should grab the nearest takeaway or easily unwrapped snack! See the tips for planning ahead (page xxx).
- Have snacks and drink with you for in the dressing room, just before and during a match or training.
- Refuel, refuel and refuel. Want to play well next time? Then it is important you restock your glycogen and energy levels promptly. The body does this best within a couple of hours after you have stopped playing. Your body wants to refuel, so help it out. See the section on refuelling and post-match snacks (page 164) to find out what's best to eat.
- Make sure you are keeping yourself well hydrated. See the section on fluid (page 173).

Tips for planning ahead

Being organised and planning ahead will mean kids can still eat well and maintain a high level of fitness and performance. This may involve you more if you are a parent and therefore good old 'Chef Mum' or 'Chef Dad'!

Food shopping

Think about the week ahead – what training and matches do the players have on? Take this into account when you do your food shopping. If the food you need for a packed lunch or a meal before you leave is in the cupboards, it avoids a last-minute dash to the shops, making do or having no other choice but a takeaway.

Packed lunches

If you give your children a packed lunch, e.g. you leave home at midday for a 3 o' clock kick-off and they will eat lunch in the car, make them varied, tasty and interesting.

Include plenty of carbs, but also a variety of foods to provide them with a balanced meal. Include a food from each of the five food groups on the Eatwell Plate to achieve this, as suggested below.

PACKED LUNCH FOR A MID-AFTERNOON KICK-OFF

- 2 pitta breads (starchy group)
- Chicken and salad filling (protein and fruit/veg group)
- A peach/nectarine (fruit/veg group)
- A yoghurt (dairy group)
- A fun-sized chocolate bar (high-fat and sugar group)
- A bottle of water

or

- A large granary roll with cheese and pickle (starchy and dairy group – the cheese will also provide protein)
- A packet of crisps – choose lower-fat varieties (high-fat and sugar group)
- A banana and a bunch of grapes (fruit/veg group)
- A bottle of water.

Planning for meals

Plan what and where your player(s) will eat after a match. Take snacks with you for refuelling straight afterwards. Packed lunches are useful as a teatime meal if you have been able to have a main meal at lunchtime. If you need a meal on the way home, try restaurants where you have more options to choose a high-carb meal, but without all the fat, e.g. a roadside chain restaurant instead of a takeaway-style burger chain or fish and chip shop.

If you are having a meal at home, a high-carb meal is essential. This does not just mean pasta. Try a jacket potato and baked beans, chilli con carne (packed with kidney beans, mushrooms, onion, garlic and tomato) or chicken with rice, plenty of new potatoes, carrots, broccoli and peas.

Pack a food bag

A cool bag is useful to keep your food fresh. It will keep your snacks, drink and packed lunch in one place and ensures you have packed all you need.

Fluid

Make sure you have enough fluid with you for before, during and after a match or training.

Eating out and takeaways

We have already touched on how you should avoid burger bars and fried chicken outlets after a match or training, but if you do have a meal out or a takeaway as a treat at other times, there are choices you can make that would be better than others. The table below gives you some ideas. Websites and instore leaflets will also give you the nutritional information for the foods that are sold, especially in chain restaurants like McDonald's, Burger King, and KFC etc.

There are many cuisines to choose from today and this table should give you a feel for what choices are better. You can then apply this to other cuisines not mentioned. Think of the way it has been cooked – Has it been deep-fried? Are there any high-fat ingredients?

Cooking tips

Food choices are all-important when you are creating a balanced diet, but these choices can soon become undesirable if they are cooked in a way that adds lots of unwanted fat. Likewise, less healthy choices can nevertheless be

TABLE 4.6	THE LESSER EVILS IN FAST-FOOD RESTAURANTS	
TYPE OF CUISINE	**WHAT TO CHOOSE** ✔	**WHAT NOT TO CHOOSE** X
Burger and chips	Plain hamburger Small portion of chips Chicken nuggets Diet drinks Salads, but watch the high-fat dressings Fruit juice Fruit Wraps – watch these, as some can be very high in fat and calories	Cheeseburger Large burgers – quarter-pounder, double burgers, burgers with bacon, lots of mayonnaise etc. Large or extra-large portion of chips Potato wedges Fruit pies Milkshakes Ice-cream desserts Normal fizzy drinks
Italian and pizza restaurants	Plain garlic bread Dough balls, but watch how much garlic butter you dip into Side salads – watch the dressings Smaller, thin and crispy pizzas Diet drinks Watch the pizza toppings – try tomato, vegetable, ham, mushroom, pineapple, chicken, seafood Pasta with tomato and vegetable sauces	Garlic bread with cheese Large deep-pan pizzas, especially the ones with the cheese in the crust Watch the toppings – avoid salami, pepperoni, spicy beef, extra cheese Pasta with creamy or cheesy sauces. Meat-based sauces can also be high-fat Normal fizzy drinks

Indian restaurants and takeaways	Chicken tikka Tandoori chicken Dry curries and tomato-based sauces Dahl Rice Chapati Naan bread	Onion bhajis Samosas Cream-based sauces, e.g. korma
Chinese restaurants and takeaways	Chicken, vegetable or prawn chop suey Stir-fried vegetables Boiled rice Boiled noodles	Crispy duck Sweet and sour balls Fried rice Fried/crispy noodles Prawn crackers
Mexican restaurants	Bean burrito Tortillas Fajitas	Tortilla chips Loaded potato skins with bacon, cheese, sour cream etc. Chimichangas
Steak restaurants/ American diners	Grilled meats Salads Jacket potatoes Rice	Fried foods, e.g. scampi, garlic mushrooms Creamy meat sauces Creamy salad dressings and dips Puddings

improved by the way we cook them, e.g. grilling sausages instead of frying them.

Here are some pointers to ensure that your food stays a healthy choice or is improved. Remember, if you use fat for cooking, consider what type it is and how much you use.

These cooking methods can apply to any food e.g. meat, fish, vegetables and fruit.

There are also ways that you can make a food healthier before you cook it, e.g. trimming the fat from meat, taking off the chicken skin, and so on.

TABLE 4.7	COOKING METHODS	
DESIRABLE METHODS ✔		**UNDESIRABLE METHODS** X
Steaming Boiling (With vegetables, don't overcook them or you will lose all their vitamins) Grilling Baking Poaching Stir-frying		Roasting Frying

Family as role models

There are many factors that dictate what children eat. These range from taste – their likes and dislikes – to peer pressure, advertising, wanting to show independence by making their own choices and the set-up for eating at home. We can all be role models to help ensure our children eat well. Older children can also be a role model to siblings and other younger children.

Meal times are family times

Eating together as a family will have a huge influence on a child's dietary intake. Here are some tips for ensuring successful meal times:

1. Sit at the table together for a meal without distractions. Turn off the radio, TV etc. and avoid texting, answering the phone or reading at the table. Avoid eating in relays, on the sofa or in front of the TV.
2. Meal times should be relaxed, social times. It is an opportunity to catch up with each other and share your day. Ask your child to tell you what went well today or what was one good thing about today.
3. Set an example with table manners.
4. Involve children in food preparation, cooking and laying the table.
5. Avoid conflict at meal times, especially over food. Do not get into a battle if your child will not eat a certain thing.

6. Praise children for what they have eaten rather than getting cross about what they haven't.
7. Offer encouragement and, if needed, sticker charts for younger children which can work towards a non-food reward over a week, e.g. a magazine or money towards something they want.
8. Keep offering new foods and a variety of foods. We need to try new foods several times before we gain a liking for them.
9. Have a family meal where you eat the same thing. Avoid cooking two or three meals every night. Children, especially young children, are far more likely to eat foods if the whole family are enjoying them together.
10. If you cannot always eat together each evening, decide on days that will be your family mealtimes. Ask the children what they would like and involve them in the decision process. You may want to give them choices!

Food labelling

Reading the nutritional information and ingredients list on a label will give you information that will help guide your food choices.

Nutritional panel

Table 4.8 will help you when looking at the nutritional information on a label to make healthier choices. The table shows us when a food contains a lot of something and when it contains a little of it. Foods containing amounts that fall in the middle contain a moderate amount.

TABLE 4.8	ASSESSING NUTRITIONAL INFORMATION ON LABELLING	
NUTRIENT	**THIS IS A LOT (PER 100 G)**	**THIS IS A LITTLE (PER 100 G)**
Fat	20 g or more	3 g or less
Saturated fat	5 g or more	1.5 g or less
Salt	1.5 g or more	0.3 g or less
	(0.6 g sodium)	(0.1 g sodium)
Sugar	15 g or more	5 g or less

Source: The Food Standards Agency

When comparing foods, use the 'per 100 g' column on the label rather than the 'per portion' column. The 'per portion' column will tell you how much of a nutrient you are getting in one product rather than another, if you were to eat that exact amount, but will not necessarily tell you which one is the highest or lowest overall. Figures need to be compared on the same portion size, e.g. 100 g versus 100 g.

You do not need to avoid all foods that contain a lot of something 'bad'. These are guidelines giving you a feel for which foods are high and which are low. It does not mean that you need to avoid all foods that contain something in a high level. It is the overall balance of your diet that is important.

Ingredients

The ingredients listed on a label are in descending order, with the biggest ingredient first. This can also give you a guide as to whether a food is high or low in something.

Nutritional claims

There are many claims that do not have an agreed legal meaning. They do however give an understanding of what the product may be, e.g. 'helps maintain a healthy heart' or 'light'.

Manufacturers cannot make misleading claims, but it is best to look further on the label. Look at the nutritional information and compare it to the table above.

Traffic light labelling

There are a growing number of supermarkets that are now including traffic light colours on the front of food labels. This tells the consumer at a glance if it is a healthy choice or not and can take away all the reading and assessing for yourself. It also helps you compare products at a glance as well as assess individual ones.

The traffic light system will tell you if the food is high, medium or low in fat, saturated fat, sugars, salt and calories. The information is presented differently in different supermarkets, e.g. as a pie chart or a table. Each nutrient will be given a colour, so you will see a mixture of colours. Try to choose foods that are predominantly green and amber. See below box for detailed breakdown of the colours.

Considerations when a player is injured

If you are injured, it is still important to maintain a balanced diet to help the body heal and recover.

If you have a muscle injury, it is important to make sure you are having enough protein for the muscle to repair itself. Eating two main portions of protein each day, e.g. meats and fish, with extras from milk, yoghurt, etc., will ensure that a player gets all they need.

If a child has an injury to a bone, e.g. a broken leg, then ensure they are eating lots of good sources of calcium. This will help strengthen the bone and aid recovery.

If you want to avoid too much weight gain or the player becoming unfit while they are injured, watch their fat intake, portion sizes, extra snacks, etc. They may have burnt this off before, but with a lower activity level they do not need as many calories.

Fluid for footballers

Why is fluid important?

As you exercise during training and playing games you will lose fluid. This fluid loss is mainly through sweat, though as we discussed earlier, younger children sweat less than older kids and adults.

The length and intensity of the exercise will dictate how much players sweat. Hot and humid weather conditions will mean that they sweat more, and the more you sweat, the more fluid your body loses. The body is sweating to cool itself and it needs to cool itself because working muscles are producing lots of heat.

If a player is not well hydrated at the beginning of the exercise and/or does not 'top up' enough during and after exercise, dehydration can occur. Being dehydrated can mean that children are not at their best. Their level of performance may slip, together with their concentration. Poor concentration levels can mean they make inaccurate decisions about tackling, saving and passing on the pitch. Dehydration in the extreme can mean that they could suffer with heatstroke.

Assessing hydration level

An indication of hydration level is the colour of your urine. Dark urine will mean you need to drink more, as you are not well hydrated. Pale yellow urine will mean your body is well hydrated. It is a good idea when children go to the toilet that you mention that they check the colour of their urine to make sure they are drinking enough.

Assessing how you feel is also a useful way to detect if you are hydrated well enough. Feeling tired and having a headache can be signs that you need to drink more, so listen out for complaints from children about these things.

Thirst is a poor indicator of hydration and by the time you feel thirsty your body is dehydrated.

Concerns over sports drinks

There is very little evidence as to whether or not sports drinks are safe or of any benefit for children under 16 years.

Some sports drinks contain caffeine, which is a stimulant and something that is unsuitable for children, especially those who are quite young. Caffeine also makes you pass more urine and then the fluid is not being used to hydrate the body. Sports drinks can contain many other ingredients apart from glucose that are either not suitable for children or in amounts designed for adults.

Tooth decay is also a concern with children. Sports drinks can have a high level of glucose in them, and fizzy varieties will be acidic, so both are concerns with dental health.

Sports drinks should not be used as ordinary drinks. If they are to be used, they should be kept to just before, during and immediately after exercising.

What to drink

The fluid you need to drink should aim to

1. replace the fluid you have lost during exercise through sweat
2. provide glucose for initial energy and energy replacement, depending on when you drink it.

Sports drinks contain sodium, which helps replace the salt lost in sweat and also aids hydration in the body. However, these are in amounts designed more for adults. You can have a go at making your own sports drinks (see box). This is also a lot cheaper if you have a whole team to hydrate!

What should children drink?

· Water, especially if they have not lost that much sweat and therefore salt
· Fruit juice and water mixed together in equal quantities
· Original squashes, diluted
· Ready-to-drink juice drinks e.g. Capri Sun, Fruit Shoot and Five Alive
· Homemade sports drinks (see box)

MAKE YOUR OWN SPORTS DRINK

Each makes a litre (1000 ml):

1. 500 ml of fruit juice plus 500 ml of water, with a pinch of salt
2. 100 ml ordinary squash plus 900 ml of water with a pinch of salt.

Remember:

· Exercise increases the need for fluid and this fluid is in addition to the six to eight glasses per day mentioned for good health.
· Players must drink before, during and after exercise.
· Take into consideration that salt and glucose can be obtained from the snacks that kids eat before, during and after exercise.
· Drinking and keeping hydrated is easier when you like the drink!
· Don't wait until players are thirsty.
· Don't let them drink so that they feel bloated and uncomfortable.
· Ask them to assess how they feel and check the colour of their urine to determine how hydrated they are and whether they need to drink more.
· Drinking little and often during the day maintains a well hydrated state.

Seeking professional advice

If you have any queries about children's health and need any medical support, then always seek out professional advice. Your GP can refer you to a healthcare professional and will also know about who is working privately in your area.

There are many dietitians who work privately. They will be able to take the information in this book one step further by assessing diet, lifestyle, exercise routine and nutritional requirements to personalise the advice to you.

Just one last point – 'nutritionists' and 'dietitians' are two different specialisms! To find out about a dietitian working privately near you, to check that a dietitian is registered or for a list of accredited sports dietitians, check the websites in the 'Useful websites' section at the end of this book.

For some sample menus, please see Appendix II on pages 190–200. For nutritional and dietary case studies, please see Appendix III on pages 201–5.

5 PUTTING IT ALL TOGETHER

In this last chapter, we give you some final pointers and advice about training and playing football with children, based on our experience and others', before we move on to drawing together the information in this book into a cohesive, easy-to-follow programme.

Psychology of football with children

This is an area where football is taking further steps to improve the mental strength and characters of children.

Football psychology is not our specialist area, but we are aware of its importance in football overall, at whatever level of football you are involved in. It is clearly an untapped and undertrained area.

For us, this is summed up in Jerry Lynch's book, *Creative Coaching*, when he states, 'It takes time to train the mind... Like a muscle, the mind needs to be stretched and exercised daily if you want to develop it and make it strong.'

So why do we not start this at an early age? One reason is that a high degree of discipline is required to apply this, and – at the risk of sounding like a broken record – kids' football is supposed to be about fun.

But football does have a big part to play when it comes to the mental attitude of our children. So, if we start with mental training 'a little and often', encouraging them all the time, giving them confidence, making football drills tough for them occasionally, getting them in better physical shape and not pampering them too much, surely our young adults of tomorrow will be of good character and strong-but-fair in mind.

Ipswich's Danny Haynes and Danny Pugh of Stoke in the thick of the action

Overtraining/overplaying

There are times when too much training or too many games can have a detrimental effect on performance. This is called 'overtraining syndrome'.

There are many symptoms of overtraining syndrome – over 90 have been identified. Here are some of the easier ones to detect in children:
- not enjoying football training
- not enjoying playing games
- feeling fatigued and listless all the time
- greater susceptibility to illness
- mood swings
- feeling anxious and stressed
- lack of sharpness.

Keep an eye out for any of the above, but also bear in mind that these could be attributed to other factors in a developing child (hormonal changes, etc.).

Why do children drop out of sport?

It is important that, as parents, teachers or coaches, we know why children might drop out of football. Below is a simple summary based on the study carried out several years ago by Michigan State University on childhood participation in sports.

The study, by Martha Ewing and Vern Seefeldt, included 10,000 students. The results showed that 45 per cent of 10-year-old children participate in sports. However, by 18 years old the number of participants falls to 26 per cent, meaning an almost 50 per cent 'dropout' rate. Why? According to the survey, the most important reasons children stop playing are:

· I lost interest
· I was not having fun
· It took too much time
· Coach was a poor teacher
· Too much pressure
· Wanted more sport activity
· I was tired of it

SAFETY AND WELFARE OF CHILDREN

As managers, coaches and conditioners – indeed, if we are involved in any capacity with junior football – we have a duty of care to young players (those under 18 years of age) while they are under our supervision. Of course, this is a moral responsibility, but it is also worth remembering that this is also a legal duty.

You should ensure that everyone can take part in an enjoyable and safe environment – the aim is to create a culture and atmosphere in which children and young people can have fun and take part safely.

There are a number of best practices and guidelines available from both the FA and the NSPCC, covering issues such as abuse, bullying, equal opportunities and discrimination.

We would also recommend that you attend the FA workshop on Child Protection and Best Practices. Even if it is only for peace of mind, it is well worth the time invested. See www.thefa.com for more details.

Further reading and advice can also be found in *Coaching Kids' Football* by Stuart Page, published by A & C Black. This covers all areas of safety, moral responsibility and current schemes to encourage participation in football.

Advice on first aid and injury treatment, compiled by Matt Byard, the Ipswich Town FC physio, can be found in Appendix 4 on pages 206–210.

- Needed more study time
- Coach had favourites
- Sport was boring
- Overemphasis on winning.

The only other reason we would add to this is that there are more distractions for our children today, like computers, and satellite or cable television channels that now have wall-to-wall coverage for children's programming.

Planning

Planning for children and young adults is almost the opposite of planning for adult amateur players – time is on your side. In fact, you have years to develop the separate components of conditioning.

Young players will not be fully physically developed until their late teens or early twenties, so enjoyment of the game must be the main priority. As discussed in Chapter 2, planning for conditioning takes a less important role – generally speaking, well organised football training will allow younger players to improve their fitness.

As we have seen, some of the components of conditioning are not a priority but can still be visited occasionally, so you should concentrate on components like running techniques (speed), body movement, suppleness and agility and basic techniques for strength work, thereby laying the foundations for the future. Stamina work for younger players tends to come just by playing the game.

Why plan?

The older children get, the more relevant planning becomes, to improve conditioning components and avoid injury and burnout.

It may seem that with more time and fewer areas of conditioning to be concerned about, planning for this group is less of an issue. Think again. It becomes more important – not only do you need to plan the season for the team, but you also need to plan for individuals as they grow and mature at different rates and keep one eye on the years ahead and how your plans now will affect the future. Added to this, with some areas of conditioning being 'off limits', e.g. weights work, you have the additional task of keeping training fresh with fewer drills to choose from.

Our analysis (over a two-year period) shows that when a boy goes through a growth spurt (growing several centimetres over a few months) it tends to affect his performance during training and matches and he may be prone to injuries, so you need to note where this is happening and make provision in planning wherever possible.

In short, no matter what the team you are responsible for, planning is your first duty!

Planning is also absolutely essential because it sets the standards that you expect of your players early on and will provide strong foundations for the team's performance during the season. Any team needs to have a clear football plan and conditioning plan if you are to have any kind of success in getting the kids to enjoy themselves over the season. In other words, any team that wants to do well must ensure the players enjoy themselves but also learn in a structured way over the course of a season.

The plan is essential as it will allow you to:
- Develop a balanced programme (see page 184)
- Vary training loads throughout the season
- Aid Rest, Recovery, Refuelling and Rehydration
- Achieve enjoyment, week in, week out
- Look after vulnerable individuals
- Achieve variety when required
- Avoid overtraining and burnout
- Avoid boredom.

The importance of planning is obvious when you see it written down, but it is often overlooked, particularly by coaches or teachers who are having to juggle a number of other priorities. If you find yourself in this situation in your capacity as a coach, parent, teacher or other helper, it is your duty to champion the cause of long-term planning in training. Sure, it may take up more time now – planning for a whole season is not a simple task – but it *will* head off problems in the future, namely the sort of problems that you won't want to deal with in the middle of the season, like injury and disillusioned players dropping out.

There is a classic saying in project management which you might already have heard, and it should be the mantra for any conditioning coach – 'failing to plan is planning for failure'. Effective player conditioning is not achieved overnight and doesn't happen by itself. It is a gradual process taking weeks and months before the results are there for all to see. And when working with elite children and elite young players it can take years of careful planning and training to get the player where they need to be. However, it is not totally necessary for you to do that, because we are unlikely to be working with elite players.

If time is limited, a lesser version of planning is to remember what you did the previous session and plan in advance what you are going to do in the next session. Always have an aim and goal for each month, as this will help you plan throughout that month. It is probably the simplest way of doing it and, if you are really pushed for time, is better than nothing.

Influencing factors

There are many factors that will influence your planning, such as games, enjoyment and morale of players – these factors rarely exist in isolation and are often interlinked. For example, the team may be on a losing streak and, as a result, morale might be low – here you would want to change the training that you are doing to freshen things up and break the routine. You need to be aware of the factors which influence your planning and be prepared to change your plans – just because you have written your plan does not mean that it is set in stone.

Factors that may influence your season planning include:
- The coach's requirements
- Your goals and aims as coach
- Feedback from the players – what do they enjoy? What's too hard?
- Fixtures and fixture congestion
- Feedback from the parents
- Facilities
- Time of year
- Most importantly, realism – design a plan which you can keep to!

Factors that might lead you to change your plans during a season include:
- Players' body language and attitude – what is it telling you?
- Players' verbal feedback
- General morale of the players
- Weather conditions
- Coach's requirements (these invariably change as the season progresses)
- Results on the pitch (although in an ideal world this should not influence the conditioning plan).

Give particular attention to the players – they can soon get bored. If possible, be sure to change location and the methods that you use to keep them interested.

Samples of a session plan structure can be found in Appendix I on pages 184–189.

General teaching principles

We've already discussed some rules to bear in mind in the coaching section in Chapter 3 (pages 101–146), but here are some more principles you might find worth noting:

- **Do the simple things well** – Remember the basics: tackling, dribbling, passing, shooting and out-thinking your opponents. They should run at different speeds, turn, explode and enjoy themselves in the process. Do not overcomplicate conditioning.
- **Do them often, with variety** – Sprints with a rugby ball and simple passing drills are always popular, so mix it up and use your imagination using the drills in this book.
- **Do them accurately with specificity in mind** – With fitness, many drills can be done using a ball. With the coaching drills in Chapter 3, use the dimensions of a kids' pitch.
- **Do them in such a way as to make a direct impact on the performance** – Most young players' passing will be on the ground, most sprints will only last a few seconds, and so on.
- **Revisit, revise and re-assess when necessary** – Never take drills or your knowledge for granted!

We hope you have enjoyed reading this book and will find what you have read so far, and the following appendices, useful when you are introducing fitness to your kids. Good luck with your programme!

'Enjoy training, enjoy football, enjoy playing with your friends, enjoy everything to do with football. Play for the enjoyment, but when your parents or coach give you advice, trust them and learn from it.'

Pablo Counago, former Spanish U21 international, with over 50 goals in the Championship and La Liga

APPENDIX 1:

Sample session plans and programmes

SESSION PLAN A – AGE 7 – 12.			
COMPONENT	ACTIVITY	DURATION	PAGES
WARM-UP	Warm-up drill 4	8 – 10 mins	12
	Strength drill 2, 3, 4, 5		37 – 41
	Strength drill 1		36
MAIN ACTIVITY	Speed drill 12	5 mins	94
	Drill Basic skills 1	30 – 40 mins	106
	Drill T&S skill 5		120
	Drill T&S skill 6		121
COOL-DOWN	Cool-down	5 mins	4 – 5
	Compliment the players		

SESSION PLAN B – AGE 7 – 12.			
COMPONENT	ACTIVITY	DURATION	PAGES
WARM-UP	Warm-up drill 1	8 – 10 mins	6
	Strength drill 1, 2, 6, 7, 8		36-7, 42-4
	Strength drill 5		40
MAIN ACTIVITY	Speed drill 10	5 mins	91 – 2
	Drill Basic skills 1	30 – 40 mins	106
	Drill T&S skill 2		117
	Drill T&S skill 9		124
COOL-DOWN	Cool-down	5 mins	4 – 5
	Compliment the players		

SESSION PLAN C – AGE 7–12.			
COMPONENT	ACTIVITY	DURATION	PAGES
WARM-UP	Warm-up drill 2	8–10 mins	8
	Strength drill 1, 2, 9, 10		49, 50, 57, 58
	Strength drill 8		44
MAIN ACTIVITY	Speed drill 2	5 mins	81
	Drill Basic skills 3	30–40 mins	108
	Drill T&S skill 1		116
	Drill T&S skill 10		125
COOL-DOWN	Cool-down	5 mins	4–5
	Compliment the players		

SESSION PLAN D – AGE 10–15.			
COMPONENT	ACTIVITY	DURATION	PAGES
WARM-UP	Warm-up drill 3	8–10 mins	10
	Strength drill 1, 2, 5, 9, 10		49, 50, 53, 57, 58
	Strength drill 2		37
MAIN ACTIVITY	Speed drill 4	5 mins	83
	Drill Basic skills 4	30–40 mins	109
	Drill T&S skill 7		122
	Drill T&S skill 8		123
COOL-DOWN	Cool-down	5 mins	4–5
	Compliment the players		

SESSION PLAN E - AGE 9-12.			
COMPONENT	ACTIVITY	DURATION	PAGES
WARM-UP	Warm-up drill 5	8-10 mins	14
	Strength drill 1, 2, 5, 6, 7		49, 50, 53, 54, 55
	Strength drill 3		38
MAIN ACTIVITY	Speed drill 8	5 mins	88
	Drill Basic skills 5	30-40 mins	110
	Drill T&S skill 11		126
	Drill T&S skill 12		127
COOL-DOWN	Cool-down	5 mins	4-5
	Compliment the players		

Sample four-week programme A for ages 7 – 15

Sample four-week programme A for ages 7 – 15				
	WEEK 1	WEEK 2	WEEK 3	WEEK 4
MONDAY	Session plan A	Session plan B	Session plan C	Session plan D
	Menu 8	Menu 9	Menu 10	Menu 8
TUESDAY	No training	No training	No training	No training
	Menu 1	Menu 1	Menu 1	Menu 1
WEDNESDAY	No training	Practice game	No training	Practice game
	Menu 2	Menu 4	Menu 3	Menu 5
THURSDAY	No training	No training	No training	No training
	Menu 3	Menu 3	Menu 1	Menu 2
FRIDAY	Practice game	No training	Practice game	No training
	Menu 5	Menu 2	Menu 4	Menu 3
SATURDAY	Match	Match	Match	Match
	Menu 6	Menu 7	Menu 6	Menu 7
SUNDAY	Rest	Rest	Rest	Rest
	Menu 2	Menu 3	Menu 2	Menu 1

Sample four-week programme B for ages 7–15			
	WEEK 1	WEEK 2	WEEK 3	WEEK 4
MONDAY	Session plan A	Session plan E	Session plan A	Session plan B
	Menu 8	Menu 9	Menu 10	Menu 9
TUESDAY	No training	No training	No training	No training
	Menu 3	Menu 1	Menu 1	Menu 2
WEDNESDAY	No training	Practice game	No training	Practice game
	Menu 2	Menu 5	Menu 3	Menu 4
THURSDAY	No training	No training	No training	No training
	Menu 1	Menu 3	Menu 2	Menu 1
FRIDAY	Practice game	No training	Practice game	No training
	Menu 4	Menu 2	Menu 5	Menu 3
SATURDAY	Match	Match	Match	Match
	Menu 7	Menu 6	Menu 7	Menu 6
SUNDAY	Rest	Rest	Rest	Rest
	Menu 2	Menu 3	Menu 1	Menu 2

Sample four-week programme C for ages 7–15			
	WEEK 1	WEEK 2	WEEK 3	WEEK 4
MONDAY	Session plan B	Session plan C	Session plan D	Session plan A
	Menu 8	Menu 10	Menu 9	Menu 10
TUESDAY	No training	No training	No training	No training
	Menu 2	Menu 2	Menu 1	Menu 2
WEDNESDAY	No training	Practice game	No training	Practice game
	Menu 1	Menu 4	Menu 2	Menu 5
THURSDAY	No training	No training	No training	No training
	Menu 3	Menu 3	Menu 1	Menu 3
FRIDAY	Practice game	No training	Practice game	No training
	Menu 5	Menu 2	Menu 4	Menu 1
SATURDAY	Match	Match	Match	Match
	Menu 6	Menu 7	Menu 6	Menu 7
SUNDAY	Rest	Rest	Rest	Rest
	Menu 1	Menu 3	Menu 3	Menu 3

APPENDIX 2:
Sample menus

Menus for rest days

These menus can be used on days when you are not training or playing. They will fit into the Eatwell Plate (see page 155) and therefore provide children with all the nutrition they need in a day. Amounts will vary depending on age, activity level and if child is going through a growth spurt. Let their appetite dictate, as long as they are growing well and are an appropriate weight for height.

Snacks are an option in between meals – healthy choices are essential, as suggested on page 164. Always provide a drink at each meal and snack time and top up with drinks at other times in the day too. Drinks should include water, juice (no added sugar) and diet fizzy drinks.

Menu 1

Breakfast
Weetabix or Shreddies with skimmed or semi-skimmed milk
Toast (granary bread) with an olive-oil based spread and Marmite
Glass of orange juice

Mid-morning snack (optional)
Piece of fruit, e.g. a banana, an apple, 2 satsumas
OR a yoghurt
OR low-fat bag of crisps
Drink, e.g. bottle of water

Packed lunch
Pitta bread with ham, low-fat cream cheese and pickle or chutney
Bag of mixed cherry tomatoes, cucumber sticks and celery
Tub of grapes and cubes of melon
Small box of dried fruit, e.g. raisins or apricot
Drink, e.g. 'no added sugar' orange squash or lemon squash

Mid-afternoon snack (optional)

Piece of fruit, e.g. a pear or a tub of pineapple cubes
OR teacake
OR cereal bar
Drink of milk or water

Dinner

Chilli con carne, wild rice and a side salad
Banana and custard
Glass of water

Menu 2

Breakfast
Porridge, Oat-So-Simple, Ready Brek or Sultana Bran with skimmed or semi-skimmed milk
A toasted cinnamon and raisin bagel with low-fat spread
Glass of apple juice

Mid-morning snack (optional)
Glass of milk and a couple of biscuits
OR piece of fruit, e.g. an apple, a handful of grapes or 2 clementines
OR a currant bun
Drink

Hot lunch
Scrambled egg on toast (granary) with grilled tomatoes
Yoghurt on fruit salad
Drink

Mid-afternoon snack (optional)
Piece of fruit, e.g. a peach or nectarine
OR cheese and biscuits
OR piece of malt loaf/teabread
Drink

Dinner
Grilled chicken, new potatoes, carrots, peas and broccoli
Low-sugar jelly set over chopped fruit, with 1 scoop of ice-cream
Glass of water

Menu 3

Breakfast
Bran Flakes with sliced banana, OR mini Shredded Wheat, OR muesli, with skimmed or semi-skimmed milk
Crumpets and low-fat spread
Glass of pineapple juice

Mid-morning snack (optional)
Smoothie
OR a piece of fruit, e.g. a banana, an orange
OR a small biscuit and chocolate bar, e.g. a 2-finger Kit-Kat, Twix
Drink

Lunch
Wraps with grilled chicken, salad and guacamole
Packet of crisps
Piece of fruit, e.g. 2 kiwi fruit, a pear
Yoghurt drink
Bottle of water

Mid-afternoon snack (optional)
Rice cakes, e.g. Snack-a-jacks
OR piece of fruit, e.g. a handful of strawberries or grapes
OR flapjack
Glass of 'no added sugar' squash

Dinner
Fish pie, sweetcorn, french beans and carrots
Rice pudding and strawberry jam
Glass of water

Match day menus

Menu 4 – 11 o'clock kick-off

Breakfast
Cereal, e.g. Weetabix OR Bran Flakes OR Shredded Wheat, with skimmed or semi-skimmed milk
Grilled bacon and baked beans on toast (granary)
Fruit juice

10 a.m.
Banana OR cereal bar
Water (see Fluid for footballers on page 173)

Dressing Room
Fruit Juice

11 a.m. – kick–off

Half Time
Drink, e.g. water
Mini chocolate bar

Post-match snack
Flapjack
OR teacake

Lunch
Baguette with egg mayonnaise and cress
Packet of low-fat crisps
Piece of fruit
Muffin
Drink

Mid-afternoon snack (optional)
Piece of fruit
OR yoghurt drink
Water

Dinner
Lasagne, salad and garlic bread
Fruit and ice-cream

Menu 5 – 11 o'clock kick-off

Breakfast
Scrambled egg and baked beans on toast
Yoghurt
2 satsumas
Glass of milk

10 a.m.
Smoothie OR biscuits
Water (See Fluid for Footballers, page 173)

Dressing Room
Drink
Handful of jelly babies

11 a.m. – kick-off

Half Time
Drink
Small banana

Post-match snack
Popcorn
OR malt loaf
Drink

Lunch
Jacket potato with prawns or tuna mayonnaise, and side salad
Piece of fruit, e.g. peach or handful of grapes
Small chocolate bar
Water

Mid-afternoon snack
Milkshake
OR scone

Dinner
Grilled steak, potato wedges, carrots, broccoli and peas
Fruit crumble

Menu 6 – 3 o'clock kick-off

Breakfast
Muesli OR Special K OR Sultana Bran, with skimmed or semi-skimmed milk
Warm croissant
Fruit juice

Mid-morning snack (optional)
Pear or apple
OR breadsticks dipped in low-fat soft cheese

Lunch
Chicken and tomato pasta bake, and warm ciabatta
Fruit salad with plain yoghurt
Fruit juice and water

2 p.m.
Cereal bar
OR malt loaf

Dressing Room
Drink
Small handful of chewy sweets

3 p.m. – kick-off

Half time
Drink e.g. water
Small banana

Post-match
Drink
Banana OR flapjack

Teatime
Ham and tomato rolls
Low-fat crisps
2 cocktail sausages
Strips of pepper, celery and cucumber
Fruit cake
Drink

Menu 7 – 3 o'clock kick-off

Breakfast
Porridge with sliced/mashed banana or jam
OR Shreddies with skimmed or semi-skimmed milk
Toast (granary) with peanut butter, marmalade or honey
Fruit juice

Mid-morning snack (optional)
Grapes or nectarine
OR *milkshake*

Lunch
Stir-fried pork and vegetables with noodles
Banana and custard
Fruit juice and water

2 p.m.
Handful of apricots
OR biscuits

Dressing Room
Drink
Small handful of chewy sweets

3 p.m. – kick-off

Half time
Drink e.g. water
Small chocolate bar

Post-match
Drink
Ham and grated cheese roll
OR popcorn

Teatime
Leek and potato soup with granary bread
Toasted teacake
Drink

Training day

Menus 8 and 9 are examples of a day where training is in the evening at 6 p.m. Menu 10 is for a weekend training session starting at 10 a.m.

Menu 8

Breakfast
Shreddies OR Weetabix, with skimmed or semi-skimmed milk
Toasted English muffins with Marmite

Mid-morning snack (optional)
Milkshake and plain biscuits
OR piece of fruit, e.g. a pear or pot of blueberries

Lunch (school dinner)
Fish fingers, potato wedges and baked beans
Rice pudding OR banana and custard

Mid-afternoon snack (advisable for a 6 p.m. training session)
Muffin
OR egg and cress roll
OR smoothie and orange
Drink

6 p.m. – Training

Post-training
Cereal bar
OR flapjack
Drink

Dinner (This can be in the car if you are travelling a distance)
Cold pasta salad, e.g. with chicken, cherry tomatoes, baby spinach and pine nuts
OR granary rolls with ham and cheese or turkey and salad
Packet of low-fat crisps
Teacake
Piece of fruit
Drink

Menu 9

Breakfast
Honey Nut Shredded Wheat OR Weetabix, with skimmed or semi-skimmed milk
Waffles and golden syrup/maple syrup

Mid-morning snack (optional)
Biscuit chocolate bar, e.g. KitKat, Club, Twix
OR piece of fruit, e.g. an apple and a box of raisins

Packed lunch
Grilled bacon and salad sandwich
Low-fat crisps
Fruit scone
Piece of fruit
Drink e.g. 'no added sugar' squash, diet fizzy drink

Mid-afternoon snack (advisable for a 6 p.m. training session)
Cereal bar
OR chicken and pickle roll
OR banana and *milkshake*
Drink

6 p.m. – Training

Post-training
Rice cakes
OR oatcakes
OR muffin
Drink

Dinner (This is more convenient if you live locally)
Salmon, new potatoes, peas, cauliflower and steamed spinach
Pancakes with lemon
Drink

Menu 10

Breakfast
Grilled bacon sandwiches OR baked beans on toast (granary)
Glass of milk

Pre-training
Drink, e.g. orange juice and water (half and half)

10 a.m. – Training

Post-training
Banana
Drink

Lunch out
Ham and pineapple pizza with a side salad
OR plain burger and small chips

OR

Lunch At Home
Jacket potato with coleslaw, chilli or prawns in mayonnaise

Mid-afternoon snack
Packet of low-fat crisps
OR *milkshake* and plain biscuits

Dinner
Spaghetti Bolognese with a side salad and garlic bread
Chocolate mousse
Drink

APPENDIX 3:
Nutritional case studies

Case Study A

Subject	13-year-old schoolboy
Exercise level	Football training 3 times a week
	Football match once a week
	Physical education at school 1–3 times a week
	Extra sports – Running
Reason for referral	For nutritional advice and weight management to improve sports performance. Coaches felt that losing some weight would help speed and agility.

This young boy and his mum were seen together at a consultation to assess a number of things that would enable effective and practical advice to be given. This included:

- his current diet
- lifestyle
- height and weight history
- current height and weight
- any medical conditions
- their opinion of his situation
- his motivation to change
- mum's input, in terms of shopping, cooking, encouragement and being a role model
- eating behaviour
- training and match routines with food.

Assessment
The boy and and his mum felt that he would benefit from losing some weight in terms of his overall health and his sports performance, and were motivated to change.

At this time he was at a higher weight than he should have been for his height. He was still growing and had no existing medical conditions.

His current diet followed regular meals (breakfast, lunch and dinner), but was high in fat and high-GI carbohydrates.

Aim

1. To achieve a degree of weight loss/weight maintenance while still growing
2. Improve his diet for optimum sports performance.

Education given

The boy and his mum were given education about food groups, the Eatwell Plate and the importance of carbohydrates as a fuel for football, and the correct type of carbohydrate for stamina and improved performance, i.e. low-GI.

Dietary changes advised

1. Stop eating Coco Pops and Frosties, and have high-fibre, low-GI cereals instead, e.g. Weetabix, porridge, Shreddies, Shredded Wheat, All-Bran, Bran Flakes.
2. Stop using sugar on cereal and try fruit for extra taste and sweetness, or an artificial sweetener (to be used sparingly).
3. Change white bread to a high-fibre low-GI variety, e.g. granary, multi-grain and seeded bread.
4. Stop having cream sauces with pasta dishes.
5. Stop eating mayonnaise and dressings with salads and choose small amounts of low-fat/light varieties.
6. Stop having chips, although was only once a week.
7. Stop eating pizza, although was only once a week.
8. Use less olive oil in cooking.
9. Choose lower-calorie curry dishes and have with boiled rice instead of fried. (This meal was once a week and was a family meal. Therefore the compromise that kept it in the diet was to educate them in terms of menu choices.)
10. Have a chocolate bar once a week instead of three times a week and to choose a 'fun size' bar.
11. Avoid drinking energy drinks at any time other than pre-match, half time and immediately post-match. Alternatives were also advocated, e.g. fruit juice and water drink or diluted original squash.

Outcome

The boy and his mum were seen a month later. He had lost 3 lb and had grown by 2.7 cm. Both of them were extremely pleased. A successful weight loss in adults would be 1 lb a week, so he had made a real achievement.

The boy had been more aware of his food choices and portion sizes, and had made a number of specific improvements to his diet, including:

1. Changing from sugar to sweetener
2. Reducing the amount of chocolate he had
3. Changing his cereal and bread to a high-fibre variety
4. Only having higher-fat foods occasionally, e.g. chips, pizza
5. Mum had made alternations to her shopping habits and food choices
6. Mum had used a spray oil instead of pouring oil straight from a bottle, therefore using less
7. He had stopped drinking Lucozade at other times in the day.

Case Study B

Subject	14-year-old schoolboy
Exercise level	Football training 3 times a week
	Football match once a week
Reason for referral	For nutritional advice – This boy had been told to 'get fitter' by the football coaches and to increase his muscle mass.

This young boy was by himself in a consultation to assess a number of things that would enable effective and practical advice to be given. This included:

- his current diet
- lifestyle
- height and weight history
- current height and weight
- any medical conditions
- his opinion of his situation
- his motivation to change
- mum's/family's input in terms of shopping, cooking, encouragement and being role models
- eating behaviour
- training and match routines with food.

Assessment

Case Study B had taken it upon himself to deal with the situation. He had reduced his food intake and tried to follow what he knew about healthy eating. As a result of being worried and trying to achieve this alone, he had been suffering from panic attacks. He had also cut out so many foods that he had compromised his nutritional intake. He was no longer getting the nutrients he needed for growth, development and good health, let alone sports performance. He had also lost a lot of weight that resulted in him being underweight for his age and height.

His diet definitely showed a lack of nutrients, a lack of calories, too many high-GI foods and processed foods, and a lack of fibre, fruit and vegetables. On a positive note, he had started eating breakfast in the last two weeks.

Aim

1. To improve his calorie intake to achieve an ideal weight for height, and ensure successful growth and development.
2. To improve his protein intake for muscle growth and development.
3. Improve his diet for optimum sports performance.
4. Improve his diet for improved nutritional status.

Education given

The boy was given education about food groups, the Eatwell Plate and the importance of carbohydrates as a fuel for football, and the type of carbohydrate for stamina and improved performance, i.e. low-GI. Education was given about protein and ways to increase his weight in a healthy way.

Dietary changes advised

1. To eat regular balanced meals and snacks, i.e. breakfast, mid-morning snack, lunch, mid-afternoon snack, dinner, supper. Appropriate meal and snack ideas were given.
2. To include at least a pint of full-cream milk per day into his diet for increased calcium and calorie intakes.
3. To change diet versions of foods to the normal varieties, e.g. thick and creamy yoghurts instead of low-fat ones.
4. To increase his portions at mealtimes.
5. To add sauces to dinners, e.g. cheese sauce, white sauce, gravy.
6. To add knobs of butter/margarine to peas/vegetables.
7. To increase his fruit and vegetable intake.
8. If having fruit as a pudding, to add ice-cream, custard or cream.

9 To try adding sugar to cereal.

10. To increase portions of a variety of meats and fish at mealtimes for increased protein.

11. To add grated cheese to meals, e.g. on top of spaghetti bolognese, melted into mashed potato.

12. To make his own milkshakes, e.g. one banana, 200 ml full-cream milk and a large scoop of vanilla ice-cream all blended together, or to use Nesquik or Crusha to make milkshakes.

13. Change white bread to low-GI varieties, e.g. granary, multigrain or seeded breads.

Outcome

The boy was seen a month later. He had gained weight, grown well, and felt much better about his body image. He was playing well and working with the fitness coach to improve his muscle development and strength with appropriate resistance exercises.

He had also made a number of beneficial changes to boost his calorie intake, protein intake and general nutrient intake.

APPENDIX 4:
Management of sports injuries

by Matt Byard, Ipswich Town physiotherapist

In this section I make some suggestions and give advice on treating injuries your players might succumb to during training or matches. Please be careful to assess whether a child's age and development will be suited to the suggested injury treatment and rehabilitation, and if in any doubt consult a chartered physiotherapist or other health professional.

Immediate treatment

Initial first aid and management of a sports injury is the most crucial part of any rehabilitation programme. Treatment always begins as soon as symptoms present. The initial management has significant implications for the further rehabilitation.

The most important principles are simple:
1. Control bleeding and therefore limit bruising.
2. Rest and avoid any further aggravation to the injury.

When injuries occur, blood vessels are usually damaged too. As a consequence, every effort should be made to control bleeding at the site of injury. The optimum management for an injury should follow the R.I.C.E. steps:
- Rest
- Ice
- Compression
- Elevation

Rest

Rest is necessary for 24–48 hours post-injury to reduce bloodflow and swelling at the injury site. It also allows the opportunity for accurate assessment to the degree and extent of the injury. It is also worth noting that once the injury occurs, the healing process begins spontaneously. Complete rest is best ensured with the use of crutches for a leg injury and a sling for an arm injury. If the injury is not rested suitably, healing is impeded and rehabilitation subsequently takes longer.

Ice

Ice is used similarly to reduce bloodflow and decrease any subsequent swelling and/or inflammation. This is best applied when crushed and applied directly to the injured area in a plastic bag or wet towel held in place with a bandage. Other products include reusable or instant frozen ice packs and ice sprays. In addition, immersion in a bucket is often favoured for injuries to feet and ankles. It is very important that ice is not applied for longer than 15 minutes and not repeated within two hours. The depth of cooling is largely dependent on the length of time for which the ice is applied. Ice should not be applied where circulation is impaired. It is also worth noting that ice can burn and cause damage to nerves if applied for too long!

Compression

Compression with a firm bandage will minimise bleeding and inflammatory swelling. The bandage should be applied tightly, but not so much as to cause pain.

Elevation

Elevation will also reduce swelling. Resting an arm in a sling or a leg on a pillow will help. It is worth remembering that the leg should be above the level of the hips.

This current management regime is most appropriate and is in fact a contrast to advice previously given out. In the past people may have been told to use heat and massage treatment, and to continue exercise. This often resulted in further aggravation to the injury and subsequent swelling. It is essential that these be avoided immediately after an injury.

Further treatment

Further immobilisation is crucial to the management of a fracture. However, generally speaking, after the first 48 hours an active rehabilitation process can commence for muscle and ligament injuries. This approach is most appropriate because any longer will invariably have an adverse effect. An early active mobilisation approach will often decrease pain and swelling and improve motivation.

A rehabilitation programme should build up to include these steps:
· Gentle stretching
· Static exercise for specific muscle groups
· Dynamic exercise with increasing resistance within pain tolerances
· Progressive resistance training

- Balance and coordination exercise
- Functional sport-specific rehabilitation.

It is true to say that muscles will weaken almost immediately and is often significant within a week post-injury. This can deteriorate further with complete immobilisation.

In a similar way, the strength of ligaments will also reduce. However, appropriate exercise can increase the strength and stability of ligaments.

Active exercise within pain tolerances will enhance circulation. This in turn will help absorb bruising and restore strength and flexibility to the injury. It is crucial that exercise management be prescribed and appropriately supervised by a chartered physiotherapist. They will assess the injury and guide the level and intensity of exercise. This is based on the degree of pain and range of movement. They will continue to review and progress the level of exercise accordingly until the injury is fully recovered.

Static exercises

This is an exercise whereby muscles contract and relax without the joint moving or the muscle lengthening. It allows maximum muscle use, maintaining strength without affecting the injury.

These exercises take a few minutes and should be carried out daily. The routine is often in a pattern of contract, hold, relax and rest. Six-second holds followed by six-second rests are often most beneficial.

A huge advantage to these exercises is, of course, that they can be done at home and require no special equipment, and more importantly little time to do. In addition they produce very little pain or discomfort.

Dynamic exercises

In these exercises, the joint is moved against a resistance. This is often best applied with exercise equipment. This can form part of a progressive exercise programme where the resistance is increased on schedule or as muscle strength increases. The muscle will adapt accordingly and increase in strength and endurance. When increasing muscle power, exercising using low repetition and higher resistance is most appropriate. For improving endurance, higher repetition and a lower resistance are used. Development of endurance protects injury through reducing fatigue. Of course strength training must be tailored to individual needs.

Stretching

All exercise programmes should be accompanied by stretching. In the first instance, the muscle is taken to the limit of discomfort and released slowly. In every instance the largest range of movement possible should be used. Stretching is often best following a 10-second hold, 10-second rest routine. A routine such as this is likely to take about 10 minutes.

In this instance, heat may now be used before doing stretching exercises. This helps to warm up the muscle and reduce pain and/or muscle spasm. Heat packs or warm showers and baths for 15 minutes before stretching are the best methods of applying heat.

Alternatively, slow and gently dynamic movements may be performed within pain limits through the largest range of movement as possible. This routine can last up to five minutes.

Medication

In injuries that cause a considerable amount of pain, medication may be used. Often appropriate medication can allow the opportunity for early rehabilitation and subsequently early return to sport. Always consult with your doctor or pharmacist before taking any medication.

Rehabilitation

A safe return to sport is largely dependent on:
- A gradual and progressive rehabilitation programme supported by a sports coach
- Further development of sport-specific patterns and drills
- Good maintenance of a cardiovascular training programme
- An optimum dietary intake
- Mental preparation.

When the injury is steadily increasing in strength, power and flexibility, rehabilitation continues. Sports rehabilitation needs to consider that the pressure and desire to return to sport is ever-present, as is the anxiety to complete rehabilitation as soon as possible.

It is crucial that fitness be maintained during the healing and rehabilitation process. Clear attention must be given to maintaining general fitness, aerobic fitness, skill level, an adequate diet and appropriate body weight. Exercises like cycling, swimming and 'aqua-jogging' are perfect. Water-based training is used to support cardiovascular fitness while facilitating the sport-specific training patterns. This is done without any further damage to the injury.

Exercising the opposite side is now equally important as a return to sport is in sight. Jogging follows, gradually increasing pace and distance covered. Furthermore, functional sport-specific training drills and activities, which aim to restore motor skills and patterns, are next on the agenda. Exercises to improve balance and coordination complete the rehabilitation programme.

Failure to rehabilitate thoroughly may result in re-injury and/or further damage. The injury must attain its pre-injury status with regard to its full strength and flexibility before returning to full sporting activity. It is also important that the rehabilitation programme continues until fully integrated into the sport once more.

Injury is an ever-present risk for a sportsperson. Fortunately, there are appropriately qualified people to ask advice from that can suggest the most practical way in which injuries can be reduced and managed.

APPENDIX 5:
Forfeits

Throughout the drills we mentioned forfeits. Here is a brief list of forfeits you could give to your young players, remembering that a forfeit is NOT a punishment (i.e. not 100 press-ups or five laps of the pitch!). Forfeits are there to bring a bit of competitiveness into training and have a bit of fun. You can get the winning team to choose the forfeit for the losing team!

- 10 press-ups
- 10 star jumps
- 10 sit-ups
- 10 tuck jumps
- Run and get all the 'loose balls'
- Run to the goal and back (no more than 50 metres)
- Collect all the equipment in after a session e.g. cones, disks, poles etc.

BIBLIOGRAPHY AND USEFUL WEBSITES

Ewing, M. E. & Seefeldt, V. D., *Role of Organized Sport in the Education and Health of American Children and Youth,* Carnegie Corporation, 1996

Lynch, J., *Creative Coaching,* Human Kinetics, 2001

Page, S., *Coaching Kids' Football,* A & C Black, 2007

Pearson, A., *Dynamic Flexibility,* A & C Black, 2004

Websites

The British Dietetic Association
www.bda.uk.com

The Health Professions Council
www.hpc-uk.org

Dietitians in Sport and Exercise Nutrition
www.disen.org

The Football Association
www.thefa.com

INDEX